CONTENTS

YOUR CAREER IN MODERN MANAGEMENT ACCOUNTING- GETTING HIRED, PROMOTED, AND ACHIEVING SUCCESS!

PART 1: IS MANAGEMENT ACCOUNTING THE RIGHT CAREER FOR COLLEGE STUDENTS?

Introduction

Are you a life-long learner? Do you love analyzing financial data and sharing your insights? Do you enjoy collaborating with others to solve challenging problems?

If so, a management accounting career might be an excellent choice for you!

Pursuing a career in management accounting is an exciting and rewarding decision that has only become more critical to professional satisfaction and business success over time. Management accountants are everywhere and work for organizations of all shapes, sizes, industries, and regions worldwide.

Ranging from financial analysts to controllers & chief finance officers; cost accountants play at least two critical roles:

1. Providing information to executive teams to inform decisions that develop strategies to improve efficiency with limited resources.

2. Working closely with business operations, understand the cost driver behaviors that determine profitability

Management accounting professionals are positioned close to operations and influence the decision-making process where they make a tangible impact on the future of their organizations.

In fact, more than 75% of financial professionals today work in businesses as management accountants with diverse career paths such as financial analysts, accounting managers, controllers, and chief financial officers; cost accounting remains a vital and growing career path.

The demand for talented professionals is only increasing and shows no signs of slowing down. As new technology changes the field, a new generation of talent is needed.

Although college students and young professionals are often guided towards public accounting straight out of college, management accounting should hold at least equal weighting in career considerations.

With above-average wages, an outstanding work-life balance, and the ability to influence change, management accounting is a rewarding career path for students and young professionals alike.

Why I wrote this book

Most accounting books that exist today serve a very narrow focus of teaching technical skills and are primarily used by college students to learn the accounting basics. What is surprising is how few books exist to help emerging accounting professionals assess the best career path and explain the various options available.

Those books that offer career advice usually only provide high-level information on the public accounting career path. This educational gap leaves students hungry for more practical tips and information.

I have written this book to aid students in bridging the divide between debits and credits and reaching career success.

I aim to share critical lessons learned during my college experience earning a bachelor's and master's degree and then working in the industry for ten years. In fact, I'm writing this with the perspective of what I wish I knew ten years ago.

Reading this book will help you answer questions like:

- "How do I become more marketable?"
- "Which accounting path is best for my needs and lifestyle?"
- "What are the key skills and knowledge required in management accounting?"
- "Is management accounting a good fit for my aspirations?"

I've often worked one-on-one with college students in an advising capacity. Still, it will be more valuable for more people to share everything I know about accounting careers, especially management accounting here.

While this book will remain helpful to anyone in the accounting profession today, it has been written primarily for the college grad and young professional demographic to aid them in finding guidance on choosing and getting started in their management accounting career.

No matter what stage you're at professionally or academically, I'm confident this book will serve as a valuable tool for understanding what a career in management accounting looks like and entails.

This book was inspired by Jerry Maginnis's recent book on accounting careers, *Advice for a Successful Career in the Accounting Profession: How to Make Your Assets Greatly Exceed Your Liabilities.*

Who Am I?

Hi, I'm Ben Wann.

I've spent the last ten years working as a management accountant in various roles and employers within the manufacturing industry.

Beginning in 2012 as a cost accountant and currently working as an Associate Director/Operational Controller for a biotech start-up, I can count on having no less than ten managers, six employers, and seven job titles and roles during my tenure, a testament to the pace of change in today's world.

This variety of positions and roles, especially the last three, working directly with executive teams, has shown me how vital skilled management accounting professionals are to organizations.

Often, there are painful knowledge gaps around understanding cost structures and profitability. Unless a skilled management accounting professional answers these questions, I've found that organizations struggle to align their strategies to reality.

I am passionate about management accounting and want to share my insights and knowledge about this career path with others. I think management accounting does not get the love or attention it deserves, and I'm here to fix that.

-Ben

Check out my website, as well: https://benjaminwann.com/blog

IMA Exemplary Young Professional Award Winner- 2019

IMA Young Professional Leadership Experience Participant- 2017

Your Feedback Is Welcome

I am always open to reader feedback. Your comments, suggestions, and advice are very welcome and appreciated.

Send anything you like to Benjamin.wann1@gmail.com.

A Quick Favor

I greatly appreciate your reading of this book- I've had a lot of fun writing it. I believe its content can help many people find the best accounting career path for themselves.

If you find this book valuable and interesting, it would mean a lot to me if you left a positive review, reflecting on your experience.

Click here ->Link to Amazon

You can also join my newsletter and receive several valuable, free gifts here-> Link

1. What is Management Accounting?

"Life is like accounting; everything must be balanced."

—Unknown

Management accounting is the foundation of every business.

Professionals in this space provide vital information to decision-makers about how well they run their companies. Management accountants work closely with business operations to truly understand the drivers of the financials and provide insights, not facts and figures, to the people that matter.

Managerial accountants work within companies or organizations to manage and improve internal financial processes, accurately monitor costs while staying up-to-date with budget trends that may affect the bottom line, and assist company leaders by anticipating and forecasting needs before they arise.

Management accountants are sometimes confused with financial or public accountants, but clear distinctions exist. While all these professionals provide valuable services to an organization, the work and responsibilities are very different.

The distinction is that management accountants work within organizations, while public/financial accountants are external parties—the main differences between financial and management accounting are emphasized further below.

	Management Accounting	Public/Financial Accounting
Purpose of Information	Help managers make decisions	Communicate financial position to outsiders
Primary Uses	Internal managers	External users; investors, creditors, government authorities
Time Dimension	Current and forward-looking	Historical
Nature of Information	Financial and non-financial	Financial
Reporting Frequency	Ad-hoc and regular cadence	Quarterly or annually
Information Format	Information is provided in a variety of formats to meet management needs. Does not have to comply with GAAP or IFRS	Information must be provided following predefined standards such as GAAP or IFRS
Control	Information may be reviewed by internal parties	Information is reviewed by public auditors

Financial and public accountants mainly focus on more technical competencies:

- Inform external groups – such as banks or investors- about an organization's health through quarterly or annual earnings statements.
- Provide tax, compliance, and risk-assessment services
- Provide advisory/audit services to an organization.
- As a management accountant, you would typically:
- Gather information on revenue, costs of goods sold, inventory, production volumes, and cash flow to spot trends, and share insights to help your company make decisions.
- Develop relationships with operations to reveal cost and

profit drivers within financial information.

- Combine financial and non-financial data to paint a complete picture of the business and then influence others to use the information to help the organization meet its financial and non-financial goals.

What Do Management Accountants Do?

A managerial accountant is responsible for analyzing and presenting a company's financial information so that management can make informed decisions. Business leaders need timely, accurate, and comprehensive answers to pressing questions - not just yes or no responses, but genuine insights to figure out what is happening between strategy and execution and help steer the ship back on track.

The managerial accountant's work begins with developing a deep understanding of the business and industry and the associated cost and profitability drivers. They will form close relationships with department managers and employees to understand their roles better.

Management accountants have been called "the backbone" behind many organizations because they see and have access to all operational aspects of an organization; goods, services, physical assets like buildings, or machinery used to impact the business's bottom line.

The work of Management accounting varies greatly by organization, industry, and position, but the core responsibilities typically include:

- Goal Setting
- Planning
- Controlling
- Decision-Making
- Problem-Solving
- Reporting

- Business Partnering
- Data Integrity

Goal Setting

Management accountants play a crucial role in the goal-setting process by helping those in the business understand their objectives and progress to milestones once a strategy and/or budget have been decided on by top management.

Managerial accountants work with business leaders to identify the few key metrics that matter most and then ensure systems and processes are put into place to ensure that progress to goals/ metrics:

- Are forward and backward-looking,
- Are updated regularly,
- Are accurate, visible, and available, and
- Include an appropriate level of details.

When teams or individuals fall behind on their objectives, management accountants work closely with individuals, managers, and executives to understand the story behind the performance gaps and help brainstorm solutions and action plans to get the organization back on track.

Planning

Managerial Accountants share information from the business with executives about what is achievable and practical from an operational perspective to form compelling strategies and realistic plans to achieve them. This process influences and supports the creation of a long-term strategy.

Management Accountants ensure all business managers understand the plan and take meaningful action to turn these aspirations into reality. They also think proactively and put processes in place to measure progress on goals to identify and fix delays and issues before they spiral out of control.

Management accountants are vital partners for building and

carrying out strategies, plans, and budgets. The value-add here is that management accountants add quantitative and qualitative perspectives to discussions.

Controlling

A management accountant's primary role is ensuring that the business has robust controls, procedures, and processes in place to monitor performance, minimize risk, and maintain legal compliance with law and regulations.

Controller functions vary across companies due to the business's size, complexity, and industry. But no matter where they are located, controlling means overseeing a company's financial health and minimizing the odds of financial "surprises."

To accomplish good controlling, management accountants must have a strong accounting knowledge foundation to build upon. They will need to be very familiar and fluent in how costs accumulate from inception, raw materials, work-in-process (WIP), and finished goods heading out the door to a customer.

They must manage and control the costs of all manufacturing, material, labor, and overhead, support performance management, and determine inventory valuation.

Although management accountants aren't required to follow Generally Accepted Accounting Principles (GAAP) for internal reporting, they must guarantee that results are:

- Accurate,
- Complete,
- Timely, and
- Meaningful.

Apart from just reporting results, managerial accountants must be able to articulate the story behind them.

Management accountants must make complex accounting practices and policies seem logical and straightforward.

Decision-Making

Management accountants play an important role in decision-making. Management accountants are responsible for providing insights and financial information and creating custom analyses on the fly to answer pressing questions that impact an organization's profitability and long-term prospects.

Organizations usually need help with the following decisions:

- Make vs. Buy
- Optimal inventory levels
- Inventory costing treatment
- Product or channel profitability
- Break-even volume levels
- Identifying products to discontinue
- Production line theoretical vs. practical capacity throughput

There are many more possibilities, but the above points will provide a taste of what is to be expected.

Average managerial accountants will provide information quickly and carelessly.

On the other hand, great accountants who are experienced in supporting decision-making know better; they take time to test whether the inputs are reasonable, the outputs are logical, and perform deep analytical dives to validate the information they provide to others fully. They understand and explain the nuances.

Is Goat Cheese Profitable

The VP of manufacturing in my former role had a funny anecdote about his experience working with past management accountants and his distrust of them.

The story goes like this; The French VP was new to the role and the United States. He was tasked with quickly learning the business in his first few weeks and needed to report back to his bosses with a proposed long-term strategy that he would develop and undertake.

So, the manufacturing VP went to the controller and asked for an analysis to determine whether the goat cheese line was profitable or not.

The accountant returned a day later and stated that his analysis showed that goat cheese is profitable. Very profitable, in fact!

With this information in hand, the manufacturing VP went back to headquarters and outlined a new strategy for expanding the profitable goat line.

But there was a problem.

Another analyst at headquarters also performed an analysis and noticed the goat cheese was nearly always very unprofitable.

How could this be?

Embarrassed, the manufacturing VP returned to his controller and asked for a second analysis. The following day, the controller reported back to him that, yes, the goat business was unprofitable.

Perplexed, the manufacturing VP asked to sit with the controller for several hours and observe the analysis process. At the end of the session, one point was evident; the controller was leading the organization in circles with poor conclusions!

Rather than perform a holistic analysis over an extended period to account for fluctuations, the controller only performed the analysis for the most recent month at-a-time and only a portion of the entire manufacturing line!

This story might seem exceptional, but lousy information goes to decision-makers more often than you'd want to believe.

Management accountants must be diligent and deeply analytical to ensure the answers provided really answer the questions at hand.

Problem-Solving

One of the most enjoyable aspects of managerial accounting is the opportunity to ingrain deeply into a business and move beyond basic accounting tasks.

Once situated in a new role, managerial accountants are in an excellent position to observe the effectiveness and efficiency of the organization and raise awareness of operational bottlenecks. Management accounting is one of the few roles that can regularly shift from working with executives and managers to line-level employees in a single day.

Management accountants can stand out by providing quantitative and qualitative information to other stakeholders and becoming involved in root cause investigations and project management.

With access to data from the whole organization, the management accountant is primed to identify poor data and lead efforts to fix these occurrences by learning and leading process improvement workshops.

Where possible, managerial accountants are also expected to identify and deploy automation solutions to their work and those they support.

Reporting

Throughout each month and on an ad hoc basis, management accountants are responsible for generating and sharing business results.

Traditionally, reporting was done through summary reports which were printed and distributed or emailed to business stakeholders.

However, one of the significant changes in management accounting is the presence of far more dynamic, responsive, and self-service reporting through technologies like business intelligence.

This means that users can assess reporting that extends from executive summaries to complete granularity with a few mouse and keyboard clicks.

Management accountants' role here is to first work with stakeholders to understand their reporting needs and determine when, how, and what level of detail they require and document these requirements. The second step is for management accountants to work closely with the IT organization to deploy or enhance existing technologies to produce this reporting.

Management accountants must become experts in these systems and use the reporting produced to help solve business challenges and build close relationships.

Power BI, Tableau, and Excel Power Pivot are some of the leading technologies today.

Business Partnering

An effective business partner is someone who makes connections between people and between issues. They are positioned between multiple business functions, connect the dots, and add an overview financial angle to conversations.

Management accountants bring their accounting toolkit, business acumen, professional objectivity, and commercial perspective to these discussions. They are not expected to know so much about the business as to contribute insights into what can be done to improve the business performance.

However, through stimulating conversations and asking questions, management accountants can facilitate the development of insights in collaboration with business managers.

The following four activities demonstrate business partnering:

1. Have the courage to speak up, challenge managers, and hold a mirror up to the business.
2. Be able to influence people, build relationships, and communicate effectively.
3. Have the willingness to collaborate in new ways.
4. Develop the business knowledge to contribute in practical ways.

Data Integrity

As briefly mentioned in Reporting above, data integrity is essential to a management accountant's ability to succeed.

As the famous saying goes, "Garbage in, garbage out."

If the management accountant does not take steps to validate and verify the accuracy of data and ensure the processes behind the data are robust, their role will significantly diminish in value as they consistently produce reporting and insights that are false and misleading.

Working with systems, operators, and managers to get a holistic view of processes and putting controls in place is one of the first things a management accountant will do in a new role.

Wrap up

The management accountant is invaluable to their organization at all stages of the strategic management process, from being at the strategy planning "table" to driving the implementation plans throughout the organization to measuring and evaluating post- implementation results to synthesizing information and making recommendations critical in achieving results and, ultimately, competitive advantage.

Management accountants in leadership roles can see the organization as a whole and understand the relationships among the various departments.

Armed with a wealth of relevant insight, experience, and skills such as planning, analysis, information synthesis, risk management, performance measurement, decision support, and leadership, management accountants are well-positioned to create strong partnerships with others to lead the organization in successful strategic management initiatives and create sustainable competitive advantage.

Why Management Accounting is a Great Profession

Management accountants find employment opportunities in a variety of work settings and industries. Although each organization has a specific set of challenges and opportunities, small or large, public and private companies all require great accounting talent to stay in business.

Every organization out there needs a management accountant to help drive and optimize the business.

Far from the transactional work that used to define accounting a generation ago, the state of management accounting today and the outlook for tomorrow appears very bright to those in this field.

Here's what management accountants love about their work:

- Management accounting is an ever-evolving profession that provides a meaningful way to make a living and build influence at work.
- There are many opportunities to advance as your career progresses.
- Management accountants' accounting skills, business knowledge, and experience are valued in every organization, industry, and geography. Management accountants know their work is valued and appreciate respect from their peers.
- The profession offers the potential to advise or be part of a senior leadership team in any environment or industry.
- The earning potential and financial rewards can be significant. The profession offers excellent flexibility to find a career that also works for your personal and family life.

As you'll learn in this section, a career in management

accounting is not only in high demand and well-paid, but it offers many opportunities to grow professionally and personally.

Management accounting is an excellent choice for those who want a career with variety, upward potential, and visibility with upper management.

Doing Work that Matters

One of the best parts of being a management accountant is developing deep business knowledge and relationships with peers, colleagues, and executives.

Because management accountants are true partners in Goal Setting, Planning, Controlling, Decision-making, and Problem-solving, they are in the loop with significant internal developments and the most important meetings. The management accountant is trusted with valuable information and is counseled for their opinion on all sorts of matters.

On the other hand, financial accountants and consultants have a lesser degree of job satisfaction derived from developing a deep level of specific mastery and knowledge working for a single employer over several years.

Rather than knowing a lot about a few things, they know a few things about a lot. For that reason, financial accountants are usually kept at the periphery and tasked with doing basic tasks that can be outsourced when an organization hires them.

Over time, the value of managerial accountants compounds as their knowledge in the business grows, and they become the go-to source for many requests.

Career security comes with this position, as the role cannot be quickly replaced or done cheaper somewhere else with an equivalent level of quality.

No "Busy Season" Hours

Let's be straight; financial accounting vs. managerial accounting is not a "one is better than the other" comparison. To different people, they are both suitable for various reasons.

With that in mind, financial accountants in public firms and consulting environments must be aware that typical workweeks will extend to 60-80 hours in the first few years, at a minimum. With tax season, many professionals are pushed to their limits and struggle to maintain their mental and physical health.

If you don't mind working long hours for 10, 15,20 years to reach partner one day, then it could be the right call.

Management accounting typically does not have this problem.

Most organizations have standard office hours of around 40-50 a week. Sometimes an unexpected crisis or crunch period will require additional effort, which rarely leads to a prolonged sacrifice of family and weekend activities. Management accounting is far more balanced and sustainable than the alternative.

Develop In-Depth Knowledge Of Business & Operations

Because management accountants work with many other people at various levels in the hierarchy, this career path is excellent for obtaining detailed knowledge and awareness of each function. Over time, accountants can build relationships and learn from other professionals in supporting disciplines to understand how the business puzzle pieces come together.

Because accounting is central to all of the functions in an organization, professionals here have an ideal position to learn the business and connect the dots.

For example, it is not uncommon for management accountants to:

- Work with the supply chain on optimizing routes on one day,
- Spend the following day with the purchasing departments to investigate unexpected variances and plan next year's pricing estimates, and then
- After that, spend the day performing an ad-hoc analysis to determine whether a new product line should be launched.

Because of the variety of experiences, management accountants can gain a deep appreciation of the system, not silos, of business. Much of this information can only be obtained once trust and relationships are established.

Autonomy And Adding Value

Besides the regular monthly, quarterly, and annual financial close schedule, much of each month's work is at the discretion of the management accountant. While they do not get complete freedom in deciding what they will do or not, they have a range of flexibility that allows them to explore and learn.

Management accountants can often step into a new role, identify better and different ways of working, implement those changes, and then continue along to help peers or other departments work smarter. As time is saved through automation and process improvements, time can be reinvested elsewhere to free up resources, improve analysis, or solve a challenging problem.

Because management accountants are so knowledgeable about the organization's financials, their opinions and perspectives are highly valued. They are often pulled into various discussions that allow them to master the ins and outs of the business and industry.

Lead The Technology Revolution

Management accountants are also very well positioned to take a leading role in supporting their organizations' advancement to the next generation of process automation, business intelligence, integrated reporting, and machine learning.

In this fast-paced world, increasing competition and new technologies are quickly changing how we do things; businesses must stay ahead at all levels to not just survive but thrive.

As management accountants have access to an enormous volume of data from all over the organization, they should become most familiar with it.

They can learn and deploy new tools and techniques to unlock the value of the data and transform it into insights. They can also demonstrate leadership in improving how their organization generates, accesses, and uses the data.

For example, with business intelligence, management accountants can take the lead in designing dashboards for each business function that:

1. Automates activities previously done manually while
2. Providing greater insights than ever before, and
3. Adds the crucial service aspect to anticipating and solving others' needs.

Unfortunately, many organizations still lack the awareness, talent, and energy to bring these innovative new technologies to fruition. There is a large and growing gap between organizations leading with best-in-class tools and those stuck in the last generation.

As a result, management accounting professionals with strong technology aptitudes and skills are in great demand to help laggard organizations catch up. Unlike some fields where the accessible and low-hanging fruit opportunities are long-gone, management accounting is full of untouched process and system improvement opportunities.

The world of management is ever-changing, with new challenges popping up almost daily. If change and technology are exciting, consider this career seriously.

Career Outlook

According to the U.S Bureau of Labor Statistics (BLS), accountants and auditors of all types have a promising future, with job prospects projected at a 7% growth rate through 2030. With many more baby boomers retiring within the next decade, opportunities will become more available.

Management accounting is also one of the safer occupations in the economy. Boom or bust, every company needs these professionals in place to run an accounting function and close the books.

During the Covid-19 pandemic, when many organizations furloughed employees, management accountants became even more critical. Organizations need to adjust to the changing economic situation quickly, requiring business insights from trusted professionals to guide their strategies.

A key point here is that the nature of management accounting has been rapidly changing and continues to evolve. Traditionally, accountants would maintain the books and records. However, today's management accounting career requires that management accountants serve as strategic partners.

Review the steps below between the scorekeeper and strategic partner to understand the progression and expectations at each stage.

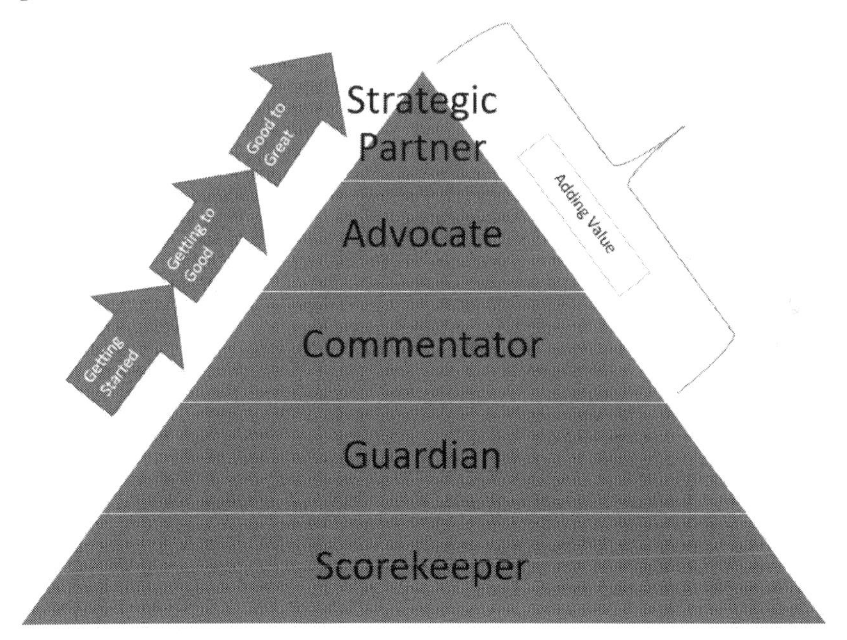

1. Scorekeeper:
    - Transaction Focus
    - Managing Costs
    - Looking Inward

- Fire Fighting
- Re-work

2. Guardian
    - Diligent Gatekeeper
    - Controls Focus
    - Manual Effort
    - Identifies and Manages Risk
    - Passive/reactive
3. Commentator
    - Balanced Scorecard
    - Clear Information
    - Includes non-financial information
    - Reactive
    - Business Aware
    - Customer Focus
4. Advocate
    - Close to the Business
    - Active on Business Teams
    - Proactive
    - Identifies Opportunities
    - Looks Beyond Finance
    - Challenges and Influences
5. Strategic Partner
    - Innovative
    - Creates Value
    - Key Management Team Member
    - Drives Opportunities
    - Thinks and Acts Strategically

Pathway To Opportunities

A management accountant typically begins their career in an entry-level position as an internal auditor, cost accountant, or financial analyst.

After a few years of experience, a management accountant may manage a team, become a financial controller, or advance as a specialized individual contributor. A few more years after that, they can become controllers for larger organizations, Head of FP&A, Director, VP, or CFO.

Below are some of the most common roles and their descriptions:

Cost Accountant

These management accounting professionals use cost accounting to review costs and help companies operate efficiently and stay on track with strategic plans. They work on budgeting, analysis, inventory, and costing models to aid in cost and risk management.

Financial Analyst

Financial analysts use market trends, forecasts, budgets, and other financial and economic information to create financial models that aid in decision-making. These models are meant to predict the outcome of purchases or decisions to help businesses manage their assets wisely.

Financial Analysts assist with financial modeling, budgeting, and preparing supporting schedules and forecasts. Analysts also track results and perform variance analyses.

Budget Analyst

Budget analysts create and analyze budgets to help businesses manage their finances, realize efficiencies, and increase profits.

Internal Auditor

Internal audits review financial statements and business operations to ensure all laws and proper procedures are being followed. Internal auditors present their findings and recommendations to senior leadership.

Treasurer

Treasurers are responsible for cash operations, cash forecasts, lender relationships, and corporate stock plans. They are skilled and knowledgeable in financing and hedging strategies. Treasurers manage all cash payable and receivable for a business while maintaining relationships with banks and lenders.

Accounting Manager

Accounting managers work closely with controllers and oversee all financial reporting. They also sometimes work with external auditors to ensure regulatory requirements are being met and implement changes to internal accounting practices to meet regulatory requirements

Controller

This senior leadership role typically reports to the CFO or CEO. The Controller manages the staff responsible for all financial reporting and accounting operations, including internal and external financial statements and regulatory reporting requirements. Additional priorities for Controllers include implementing internal control systems, evaluating the effectiveness of accounting systems, and monitoring business performance metrics.

Manager/Director – Data Analytics

Professionals in this role have deep knowledge of statistics, data science, data extraction, and visualization. They are responsible for analyzing raw data from across an organization, including non-financial data, for identifying trends and insights that impact business decisions.

Manager Of Internal Auditing

Managers of internal auditing are leaders who supervise internal auditing teams. They ensure the business or organization observes all necessary laws and procedures.

Manager/Director – Strategic Planning

Professionals in this role typically report to the CFO or CEO and develop comprehensive strategies for growth across a company's products and services portfolio. Their duties include scanning the external business environment to determine organic growth potential and opportunities through mergers and acquisitions (M & M&A) activities.

Financial Vice President (VP)

A Vice President of Finance is responsible for implementing

strategic financial management plans. They prioritize profitability and cost management and play a prominent role in company growth.

Vice President – Financial Planning & Analysis (FP&A)

The Vice President of FP&A leads a team of managers and financial analysts and typically reports to the CFO. They are responsible for finalizing and implementing corporate strategies that focus on profitability and cost containment. In addition, they ensure that strategic priorities and decisions are built into the planning processes across the company. Executives in this position will also play a central role in analyzing business cases for developing new markets, products, and services.

CFO

As a senior leadership team member, the CFO is a crucial advisor to the CEO. Priorities for the CFO include capital requirements for the entire business, sourcing and structuring corporate financing, maintaining relationships with lenders and investors, and evaluating merger and acquisition opportunities. The CFO often communicates with external parties such as investment analysts, regulatory officials, and news media.

Additional responsibilities of the CFO include all financial reporting and accounting operations and may include other functions such as Information Technology, Human Resources, and Facilities. A Controller typically supports the CFO.

Earnings Potential

As the saying goes, save the best for last! Let's talk money.

Many young professionals set out into the accounting world because they seek a career that will be meaningful AND also pay their bills.

The good news is that management accountants can do both as they are in high demand and are well compensated. The Institute of Management Accountants (IMA) provides an annual salary survey to assess the field and share salary insights each year.

TABLE 3: MEDIAN SALARY AND TOTAL COMPENSATION BY REGION, CMA VS. NON-CMA

	CMA		Non-CMA		CMAs as % of Non-CMAs	
	Base Salary ($)	Total Compensation ($)	Base Salary ($)	Total Compensation ($)	Base Salary	Total Compensation
Americas	110,000	124,000	90,000	99,000	122%	125%
Asia/Pacific	25,902	31,000	20,000	23,000	130%	135%
Europe	*	*	*	*	*	*
Middle East/ Africa/India	31,600	36,000	18,000	20,000	176%	180%
All Countries	70,000	79,000	45,000	50,000	156%	158%

*IMA's 2021 Global Salary Survey

From this year's report, the key insights are:

- Globally, the median total compensation is 58% higher for CMAs than non-CMAs. *
- CMAs of all ages earn more than non-CMAs. Those aged 30-39 receive a median salary 49-50% greater than their non-CMA peers.*
- 88% of survey respondents agree that the CMA gives them more confidence to perform their job at a high level, and 85% believe it strengthens their ability to move across all business areas.

While those who have only a CMA do better than those without any credential, the best option is always to get more than one and obtain as much education as is practicable.

Even if you choose to obtain no certification, you can still earn a comfortable living, as you can see from the table.

TABLE 7: MEDIAN TOTAL COMPENSATION BY AGE AND CERTIFICATION							
Age Range	No CMA nor CPA ($)	CMA only ($)	CPA only ($)	Both CMA and CPA ($)	% Difference CMA only	% Difference CPA only	% Difference Both CMA and CPA
20-29	65,500	80,000	79,925	97,250	22%	22%	48%
30-39	92,000	111,200	105,200	116,500	21%	14%	27%
40-49	101,500	129,000	145,000	156,250	27%	43%	54%
50 and older	118,500	136,000	155,175	146,280	15%	31%	23%
All ages	93,900	122,000	135,758	140,000	30%	45%	49%

*IMA 2021 US Salary Survey

Title	25th percentile	50th percentile	75th percentile
Manager of Cost Accounting	$82,000	$99,500	$115,500
Senior Cost Accountant	$69,000	$84,500	$96,250
Cost Accountant, 1–3 Years' Experience	$55,500	$67,000	$78,250

*Robert Half *https://www.roberthalf.com/salary-guide/specialization/finance-and-accounting*

Robert Half also provides an annual salary report which sheds further light on the pay ranges for entry to mid-level finance positions.

If you are interested in learning more, check out these resources when you have time. The IMA's salary survey also comes with a tool that helps you estimate lifetime earnings based on location, education, position, and seniority.

Attributes for Success

Accountants have gotten a traditionally poor reputation as introverted, bookish, and loner individuals who sit at a computer all day in a darkened office.

This could not be further from the truth.

Today, management accountants must have a diverse skillset,

eagerness to learn, and the appropriate character traits to help them succeed.

ATTITUDE

A can-do attitude is critical. There are often challenges with messy data, broken processes, and insufficient systems that must be tackled. Management accountants need to maintain positivity and an eagerness to fix the existing issues with an eagerness to support the business.

Conflict and disagreements will inevitably arise in working with different functions and people. Maintaining professional composure and attitude can help diffuse disagreements and help everyone get back on track.

COMMITMENT

Learning a business from start to finish is a challenging task. Becoming comfortable in any role typically takes at least 8-12 months and then another year or two to continue building relationships, improving the position, and demonstrating a measurable impact on the organization.

Leaving a role without accomplishing much is not a good long-term strategy that will make you more marketable in the future. For that reason, it is essential to take time to find a great employer that fits your style and to whom you can commit at least 2-3 years, ideally.

Plan to step into a role and only consider leaving once the role has been updated to modern standards and aligned with leadership's expectations.

HARD WORK

No tasks are usually beyond a management accountant. While high visibility assignments come every now and then, much of the role takes place behind the scenes and involves a lot of hard work to build a solid foundation to expand.

The initial phase of many managerial accounting roles involves digging deep into the data and sticking with challenges until they are resolved, processes are improved, and issues/errors are weeded out.

While this work is not glamourous, it pays off in the long run as automation cannot be deployed on broken processes. Over time, automation improves the daily grind, but putting this technology into place requires focus, dedication, and persistence, i.e., hard work.

INITIATIVE

One of the most exciting aspects of management accounting is the opportunity to identify challenges and volunteer to take the lead or resolve issues. The variety of work in the role exposes professionals to different perspectives that allow them to see issues and problems in a new light.

Demonstrating initiative is a much-appreciated characteristic and is also a growth accelerant. Taking on initiatives will help newcomers expand beyond the accounting basics and begin to really master the trade.

PROFESSIONALISM

A professional is a trusted and skilled worker who is emotionally balanced, demonstrates excellent judgment, understands best practices, and continually learns new skills. Professionalism is noted by a strong reputation and a high level of work ethic and excellence.

Professionalism is critical to management accounting. Because you will have access to confidential and sensitive information, you need to be trusted to never share or disclose this information outside the organization.

Professionalism is critical when dealing with others because it dictates how to act, look, and behave in various situations. It is the guiding principle that can be applied everywhere to great effect to build your credibility and image among your colleagues.

One of the keys to professionalism is keeping your word. If you say you will do something:

- Do it to the best of your ability,
- On-time, and
- Exceed expectations.

This is one of the quickest and most reliable means of building trust with your manager and stakeholders.

PERSEVERANCE

Perseverance means continuing onwards with a course of action without regard to discouragement, opposition, or previous failure.

In management accounting, this characteristic comes in handy all the time. Whether a reporting tool has an unexpected failure, a process improvement initiative must take a step backward, or executives disagree with your assessment, you must not get easily discouraged.

Many learning opportunities come from missteps, and the best professionals learn from these and adapt. Giving up and quitting will not get you far. Try your best, remain humble, and continuously strive to learn.

Learn from positive and negative experiences and apply feedback to keep growing in the right direction.

RESILIENCE AND MENTAL TOUGHNESS (GRIT)

Resilience is the mental ability to recover quickly from depression, illness, or misfortune.

Resilience is another critical characteristic in management accounting because the work is often tied to leading change. Whether an initiative is small or large, there will always be challenges, pushback, and delays that can be discouraging if you let them.

Instead, those with resilience look at challenges as opportunities with fresh eyes and do not deviate from their course (within reason). They dig in, move mountains, and produce results.

TEAMWORK

Management accounting is a team sport. This role is in the middle of the business and regularly interacts with every function. They must have a collaborative mindset to understand the needs of others to produce results.

Working as a team is a highly effective way to determine the optimal solution and build the support necessary to get everyone on board when dealing with change management.

When working with others, you can build your business knowledge and form crucial relationships that reveal the hidden and deeply valuable business insights found nowhere else.

FLEXIBILITY AND COMPROMISE

During any workweek, a management accountant will face shifting priorities. To avoid becoming overwhelmed, they must remain flexible and organized to identify the most important tasks and find other ways to delegate what cannot be accomplished.

Part of the job also establishes expectations over pace, work hours, and availability. If boundaries are not set and maintained, work will expand to fill the gap and wreak havoc on your personal life and peace of mind.

Although there is always much to do, remaining flexible and working with managers and subordinates to discuss and plan out the work is an excellent idea for staying highly effective over the long term.

EMOTIONAL INTELLIGENCE

In a management accounting role, there will be times when discussions turn heated, someone gets upset, or a misunderstanding occurs.

It's part of our human nature. What matters is how management accountants react to these situations. Those with high levels of emotional intelligence will learn to bring a human touch to their approach and know-how to diffuse situations before they blow up.

Emotional intelligence takes a long time to master and is a skill that grows through both study and practice.

Business stakeholders generally don't want reports and data tables. They need someone who understands them and their needs and can adapt to explain the story behind the numbers in a human and compelling manner.

Determine Your Interests & Fit

The next step towards a career in managerial accounting is determining if this path is the right fit for you.

Attributes of successful management accountants include:

- Ability and eagerness to learn and continuously improve.
- Able to work with ambiguity and apply information to accounting frameworks.
- Interest in working with and learning from others.
- Critical reasoning capabilities to assess inputs and outputs and identify where additional investigations are required.
- Communication skills. Management accountants must explain sometimes complicated accounting practices in a common language to non-business folks. At the same time, they must be able to present to senior leaders and executives.
- Technology aptitude. Microsoft Excel is the most common tool, including Enterprise Resource Planning (ERP), budgeting, forecasting, and procurement systems. Management accountants must become highly knowledgeable experts in this space to ensure data integrity and access to this information.

In general, you will want to have a fascination with business.

If you like to read and learn about business topics and how they impact the world, this could be the right fit for you. Management accounting is tied to all business operations. Financial performance does not focus on only a small, isolated area of mastery.

While some may think you need to be a math whiz to fit into management accounting, that is more of a myth.

Yes, you will need to do basic arithmetic, but the more critical skill set is understanding accounting principles and applying a broad discipline to specific challenges. Today, software and computer systems do complex math and calculations, and management accountants are essential in validating inputs and ensuring that processes are error-free and efficient in their calculations.

Aspiring management accountants might also look for personal characteristics that indicate a dedication to continually maintaining and developing their skills. Since a managerial accountant needs to analyze and advise, you must be dedicated to helping organizations grow and thrive.

Misconceptions

One of the common misconceptions with management accounting is an easy job with a relaxed schedule- This is very far from the truth.

Management accounting is a field where continuous development and learning are the norms. To survive in the field, you must come in with a broad knowledge base and have the interest and capacity to continue learning as you progress in your career.

Although a bachelor's degree is the bare minimum, many management accountants will pursue MBAs and multiple certifications to develop their skillsets.

Although management accountants have a balanced work-life situation, professionals must be committed to developing a schedule to read regularly, network, study, and identify new solutions.

Why I chose Management Accounting

I began studying accounting during my first year in college during the 2009 recession. At that time, businesses everywhere were laying off employees and shutting down.

But, I noticed the need for accountants never diminished. So, I changed majors and focused on studying accounting. Within four years, I graduated with a dual finance/accounting major and landed my first job in the prestigious DuPont finance rotational program in Wilmington, Delaware.

There I learned the basics, and over the next few years, I advanced into more senior roles where I could significantly impact organizations. In one instance, I was responsible for overhauling an entire costing department. Within two years, my team could satisfy all of the leadership's needs and implement a business intelligence tool that automated 10 hrs of work a day.

Today, ten years in, I've continued to advance and currently serve as a director/controller for a biotech start-up.

I enjoy management accounting because it has offered me the flexibility, salary & personal growth, visibility to management, and ability to impact that I crave. In many accounting roles, the work is mundane and repetitive.

In management accounting, each day is different, the work is interesting, and I've enjoyed a good deal of autonomy. I enjoy the comfortable pace of the work and the challenging analysis that I am trusted with.

As I consider my career over the next few years, I now have access to career paths for various leadership and executive roles.

For these reasons and those itemized early, management accounting is a strong career option for many. Management accounting is the perfect career choice for those passionate about numbers and an eye on the future.

PART 2: GETTING HIRED IN MANAGERIAL ACCOUNTING

With the economy in a constant state of flux, it is essential now, more than ever, to ensure you are doing everything possible to secure your future and land a great job after earning your degree.

One way to do this is by becoming a management accountant!

There are a few essential considerations to keep in mind and several educational requirements that must be met to become a management accountant.

But, if you take the time to understand the pathway and plan accordingly, you will not only sidestep any hurdles but also stand out from any competition in your future job search.

Landing your first job is a thrilling moment in any young person's life that signals your launch into adulthood. Reading this guide and the information below will keep the experience positive and remove stress from the equation.

The steps that will be covered in this section are:

1. Required Skills and Education
2. Optimizing Your College Experience
3. Join the IMA
4. Selecting an Accounting Credential
5. Land an Internship

Required Skills and education

Management accountants are expected to have a diverse skill set to meet the challenges they'll face in an accounting career.

Although much of what you will need to master throughout your career comes from on-the-job experience, basic building blocks are required. The skills required can be broken down into hard (things you know) and soft skills (ability to work with others).

Step	Skill Type
1. Earn a bachelor's degree	Hard Skill
2. Excel, Databases, Business Intelligence	Hard Skill
3. Relationship Building	Soft Skill
3. Relationship Building	Soft Skill

Earn A Bachelor's Degree

Management accountants must hold a bachelor's degree in accounting or finance.

A 4-year degree program provides the foundation in accounting and business concepts that cost accountants need. Accounting programs focus on developing a knowledge base of core business concepts such as computer applications, economics, business law, marketing, and management.

These curriculums also delve into accounting topics, including finance, computer applications, accounting information systems, and advanced managerial accounting. Those holding a bachelor's degree in accounting will be prepared to enter the field of cost accounting and other potentially rewarding careers in accounting and finance.

While 120 credit hours is the threshold for a degree, you can also explore adding a double major or a minor to improve your career readiness and marketability. Accounting majors with a computer science major or minor have been in exceptionally high demand in the last few years.

Excel, Databases, Business Intelligence

You will work with computers, systems, and data daily as a management accountant. And you need to eventually master these systems and find ways to extract, analyze, and present information as efficiently and effectively as possible.

Management accountants benefit from obtaining early proficiency in financial analysis, accounting, and database tools. As accounting technologies become increasingly automated, businesses need accountants who can carefully track and review the work of a computer.

It is highly recommended that you take several classes and certifications, if possible, in Microsoft Excel Coming out of college. No matter what industry or geography you work in, Excel is the workhorse of accounting.

As a management accountant, you should strive to be an expert or highly proficient in the software when you start your first day. (Being the best at Excel in an office is a fantastic way to make new friends)

Microsoft Power BI & Tableau are the market's leading Business Intelligence (BI) tools. It will be constructive if you can take a class to learn how to use the tools. Otherwise, the programs are free to download, and multiple websites provide students with access to high-quality data sets that can be explored at their own pace.

1. *https://datasetsearch.research.google.com/*
2. *https://www.kaggle.com/datasets*
3. *https://www.data.gov/*

Coding or programming courses such as R or Dax are also worth taking, which power Microsoft PowerPivot and PowerBI.

Making Connections

You must learn to form different working relationships with your future colleagues. A crucial part of management accounting is establishing solid relationships with various business stakeholders to learn about the industry and reveal hidden insights which explain financial results.

Take a course that teaches you the psychology of getting people to like you, making friends, communicating, and building trust.

You can also work on strengthening and establishing new relationships in your daily life and with peers in your community.

Public Speaking And Presentations

The outcome of any analysis completed in your future job will be to present your findings to your team, manager, or group of executives.

For many, the very thought of public speaking can strike fear and anxiety into their heart. But, like most things in life, the best way to get over the anxiety and develop skills here is to become educated and practice the fundamental skills.

Learning to speak in public and give good presentations confidently are powerful skills no matter where you work or do. In business, Microsoft PowerPoint is still the de facto presentation tool. Learn it, love it, master it.

Use your time in college to practice giving presentations in class and other events that push you to stretch outside your comfort zone.

Wrap-Up

While the above points are a great start to boost your hard and soft skills, this list is only the beginning. Reflect on your strengths and weaknesses, and then find courses or programs to help you grow personally and professionally.

It is also worth connecting with managerial accountants from your school or network who can explain the in-demand skills in more detail and explain where and how to get started learning them.

Making the Most From College Experience

While progressing through college, there are several different ways that you can take advantage of available resources to become more career-aware and prepared.

Many of these resources are often free and encouraged for undergraduates to attend. Unfortunately, many students unwisely pass these opportunities by.

Read through the suggestions below and give each one a shot. There are no downsides to becoming more involved in college; the experiences will reflect positively on you and help better prepare you for the next steps.

Join The Accounting/Finance Association

College campuses offer a variety of student organizations, clubs, and activities. Not only do they foster friendships, but club involvement enriches student resumes.

Participation shows employers you did more than the bare minimum in college. It also demonstrates that you can balance schoolwork with extracurricular activities. It also shows your ability to work with a team in many cases. Campus involvement also builds a transferable skill set you can apply in the workforce.

While studying, you should balance your time and energy between classes and become involved with student groups, especially those specializing in accounting and finance.

These groups will often break in guest speakers to talk about their careers, arrange visits to major employers, or help students build camaraderie to share tips and guidance.

Participate in Career Fairs

Most colleges hold career fairs once or twice a year to bring local employers to the school. This is an excellent opportunity to get a feel for who is hiring, what skills they are looking for, and even have your resume read by a potential hiring manager.

If nothing else, career fairs can broaden your awareness of the various types of employers who can share more about their industry. Many industries are available in management accounting, so it is always a bright idea to identify those that connect best with your interests and aspirations.

Engage with the Career Office

The career office is another excellent resource that students can use to prepare for their eventual careers. Each career office varies in its programs, but most offer workshops to prepare resumes, practice interviewing, teach the do's and don'ts of professionalism, and much more.

Career offices will also arrange interview days with local employers and share information on programs actively seeking out management accountants. Employers will frequently reach out to schools to get leads on great potential hires, and you should have your name known to them.

Prepare A Resume And Social Media Profile

College is perfect for crafting your resume and building your brand on social media. You must sell yourself and highlight your unique skills and personality to get hired.

Whether you use the Career Office, peer/teacher feedback, or workshops, you'll find no lack of resources and guidance on crafting a resume that finds itself on the top of the stack. The competition is high for your first job, so capturing your value proposition is essential.

Once a resume is crafted, you should also create at least a LinkedIn profile. Add a professional picture, add information about your college and educational experience, and start to connect with people you know. You'll find that with LinkedIn, you can form relationships that lead to potential job leads not found elsewhere.

Obtain An Internship

While not always required, internships can help students gain practical accounting experience before graduating. The best internships build real experience in cost accounting, professionalism, and organizational skills.

University career centers often help students secure full-time or part-time summer internships during the school year. Summer internships last 3-4 months, while other internships typically run a semester.

Many organizations also run rotational developmental programs just for interns. Perform an internet search to identify and apply to these programs. Students who perform very well in these internships often find a full-time offer upon graduation, which can significantly destress the process.

Essentially, internships are real-world job experiences. Finding a paid opportunity is best but be willing to accept an unpaid internship if nothing else is available.

Advanced Degrees & MBAs

Many students are often tempted to continue their educations straight away after earning their bachelor's degrees. This could be the right or wrong decision, depending on the individual.

For most, finding employment upon graduation will be the best choice. With the cost of tuition leaving many students with debts to pay, it is wise to start working and paying these debts off early.

At the same time, many critical management accounting skills are learned on the job, not in school. Adding a master's or MBA degree will make more sense in the future once you have begun working and get a better understanding of your career interests.

Once you have completed your degree in accounting with a concentration in managerial accounting, you should consider working for at least 3-5 years before pursuing additional degrees. Many top MBA programs also prefer students with at least five years of work experience.

Some students who consider the dual CPA/CMA certifications may want to plan to earn at least 150 credits in their undergraduate degree to avoid the additional costs of a master's degree later. Check your state CPA regulations for further guidance here.

Wrap-Up

Between the internships, volunteer opportunities, student jobs, and campus involvement, you'll gather various valuable skills and experiences to which employers will be attracted.

So, get out there and get a head start on your competition.

My College Experience

I started college at a two-year school and eventually transferred to Rutgers University-Camden. While at Rutgers, I earned 156 credits in anticipation of completing my CPA in the following two years. This smart move saved a lot of time and money while avoiding a specialist master's degree. That is what I did right.

Now, here is what I did wrong. I worked with my college career center to interview at various organizations. It went well, and I accepted a job offer through them. It was great; I was speechless.

But, I wasn't done interviewing and kept talking to organizations. I found a better offer and went to the career center for guidance in choosing which to accept. The woman who had helped me was livid. I had made her look foolish by now, wanting to turn down the first offer.

Ultimately, I kept the second offer, which was the right choice. But I burned a bridge. Please don't do what I did. If you receive a job offer, especially through your school, either be upfront that you are still interviewing and ask for more time or accept it and keep your word.

Join the IMA

The US-based Institute of Management Accountants or IMA is the most influential and prominent organization for management accountants. The IMA has more than 140,000 global members who work in accounting and finance.

The IMA is a fantastic resource for anything related to skills development, leadership opportunities, networking, mentorship, professional development, and industry news and publications.

With a membership, the organization offers regular online courses, local, regional, and national networking events, and various opportunities to get involved and develop leadership.

I've been a member my entire career, and nearly all cost accountants I've known have been involved.

While there are many benefits and reasons for joining, the most important to me has been that the organization strives to ensure that professionals are in tune with best practices, modern technologies, and career development.

There is so much to learn as you progress through your career and the IMA is the best organization to support your growth.

The IMA also sponsors the world-renowned CMA certification, the gold standard in management accounting.

Register To Join IMA

As a student, there are additional benefits to becoming involved with the IMA early on.

For one, as an IMA Student member, you can learn about the role of accountants and financial managers in business and explore your career options.

The IMA offers student members access to many benefits of regular Professional membership at a significantly reduced rate. You must be enrolled in 6 or more credit hours at a college or university to qualify for this membership type.

Even better, students who register and are in the know can apply for CMA scholarships while still in school. It costs nothing to apply and provides an outstanding value. As you send out your resume during the hiring process, seeing that you are currently studying for or have passed the CMA exam will indicate your high potential.

https://www.imanet.org/cma-certification/cma-scholarship?ssopc=1

Student CMA Scholarships

Who is it for?

- High-achieving students (undergrad through Ph.D.)
- Students who attend an accredited college or university in the U.S. or around the world
- 10 students per school per academic year can be nominated for a scholarship
- All students who a professor nominates will earn the scholarship

What's included?

- Entrance fee to the CMA program
- Exam support package with retired exam questions and a glossary of terms
- Registration fees covering both parts of the exam (additional fees will apply for retakes)
- Choice of course provider review material (All regions except China)
- Three years of IMA membership while pursuing the certification

Where are the application forms?

If you are a student at an accredited college or university, ask your professor to nominate you with this form. Students cannot self-nominate. Ph.D. students can apply here.

When are applications due?

IMA accepts applications from September 1 through June 30. Students must activate their scholarship within two weeks of notification from IMA.

Why should you take the CMA exam while still in school?

For various reasons, many students find it valuable and efficient to take the CMA exam while still in school. Generally, students start early because they are already in study mode and exam material is top of mind. They can take both exam parts now and submit their work experience later, allowing more time for their career after college.

1. Boosts your resume early

Before graduating, candidates who pass the CMA Exam (or one of its parts) have a valuable resume addition while applying for entry-level accounting jobs. You may have an advantage over job candidates who have not started to study for the CMA Exam already.

2. The content may be fresh after your college accounting courses

Much of the exam content is taught in higher-level accounting classes - if you start sooner, the content will be fresh in your mind.

Let's assume you take the exam a year after completing your undergraduate cost accounting course. As you study for the CMA Exam, the cost accounting topics will be familiar, and your CMA Exam prep may be more straightforward than if you'd waited until years after taking the course.

Once you start your career, you may not handle cost accounting transactions, and CMA Exam prep may be more challenging.

If you graduate having already passed the CMA Exam, you won't stress exam preparation after you're done with school. When CMA Exam prep is behind you, you'll have more time to focus on your career.

Find A Mentor

One of the reasons the IMA is an excellent choice for all students is the mentorship program. If you don't have any potential mentors in your personal network, you can use IMA's online tool that pairs mentors and mentees. You can view profiles and find the best match for you.

Complete A Career Driver Assessment

The online Career Driver Assessment is another excellent tool available to all IMA members and is especially valuable to students. This tool allows you to answer questions to honestly and accurately assess your skills, identify the best career path based on your interests and personality, and learn what a long-term career path will look like.

The tool is free to use and explore. Highly recommended.

https://www.imanet.org/career-resources/careerdriver?ssopc=1

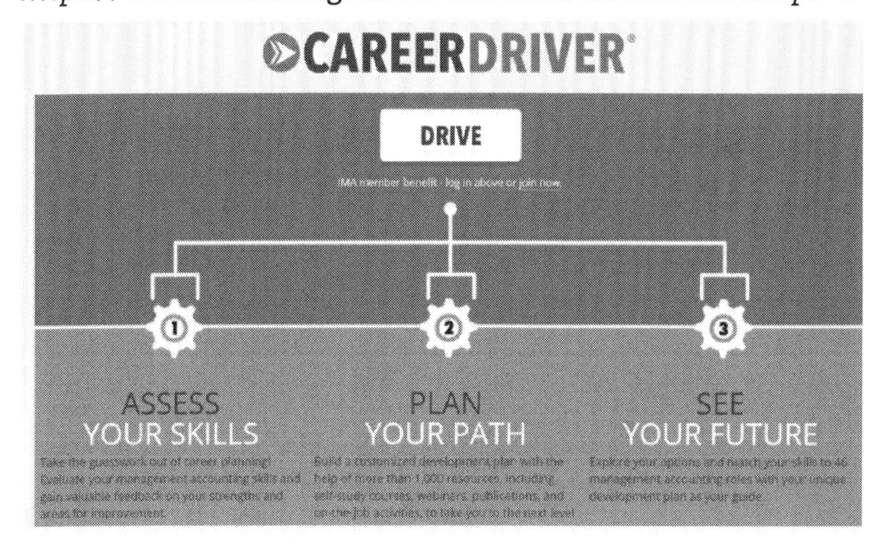

My IMA Experience

The IMA has been a valuable resource for many different aspects of my career. I've met lots of interesting people, I've found caring mentors, and I've been able to identify and apply new technologies at work by understanding industry trends.

Unfortunately, when I look back on my career, I have seen professionals who haven't excelled mainly due to losing sight of what "good looks like" and have struggled to remain relevant.

Remaining relevant and influential at work is tied to remaining informed. Management accounting has changed drastically in the last twenty years, and I'm excited about the next twenty years. Whether you choose the IMA or not, you must stay current and up to date with industry best practices.

Selecting an Accounting Credential

College is the perfect time to consider which accounting credential best suits your career aspirations. Although there are many credentials in the professional world, the CMA and CPA are the most commonly achieved.

Let's review and discuss each one.

THE CMA

While there are many different credentials out there, the CMA is the most valuable and practical option. The CMA, which stands for Certified Management Accountant, has been the global benchmark for accounting and finance professionals for over 50 years.

The CMA body of knowledge teaches accountants strategic thinking, applied work experience, and the ability to convert data into dialogue and insights into action.

One of the reasons it is highly regarded is the rigorous CMA certification process (which includes holding a bachelor's degree) and its commitment to ongoing education.

The CMA designation is recognized worldwide, and professionals who earn the certification are in demand. To specialize in management accounting and have career flexibility, you should study for the CMA certification.

The Institute of Management Accountants (IMA) provides the CMA designation, and candidates must meet educational requirements and other standards. CMA candidates must also pass both parts of the CMA Exam, covering many management accounting topics.

Becoming a CMA separates you from other accountants and enhances your other credentials. CMAs often take on management responsibilities and can advance quickly in their careers. As a CMA, you may specialize in financial analysis, cost accounting, or other areas.

The CMA requires only a bachelor's degree, the exam can be taken in college or during your career, and the certification is granted after two years of work experience.

The CMA exam consists of 2 parts covering 12 competencies.

The CMA exams

Revised in 2020 to reflect the new demands of the accounting and finance profession - tests expertise in 12 core practice areas:

External Financial Reporting Decisions	Financial Statement Analysis
Planning, Budgeting, and Forecasting	Corporate Finance
Performance Management	Risk Management
Cost Management	Decision Analysis
Internal Controls	Investment Decisions
Technology and Analytics	Professional Ethics

- 50% pass rate globally
- 4,000 CMAs granted each year on average
- 70,000 CMAs awarded to date, everyone earned through testing

Because of the challenging nature of the material and 3-distinct knowledge application levels, many candidates study for 100 hours or more to pass.

•

Part 1: Financial Planning, Performance, and Analytics

15% External Financial Reporting Decisions

20% Planning, Budgeting, and Forecasting

20% Performance Management

15% Cost Management

15% Internal Controls

15% Technology and Analytics

Part 2: Strategic Financial Management

20% Financial Statement Analysis

20%	Corporate Finance
25%	Decision Analysis
10%	Risk Management
10%	Investment Decisions
15%	Professional Ethics

CMAs between the ages of 20-29 can earn 37% more in total compensation than non-CMAs globally, according to IMA's 2021 Global Salary Survey.

Unlike the CPA, the CMA is a global certification. The CMA has brand name recognition and transferability no matter where you live or when you're from.

THE CPA

The CPA is a credential focused on the public accounting discipline of audit and tax services.

To become a licensed Certified Public Accountant (CPA), you must meet the education, examination, and experience requirements. All candidates must pass the Uniform CPA Examination ® (CPA Exam), which comprises four sections: Auditing and Attestation (AUD), Business Environment and Concepts (BEC), Financial Accounting and Reporting (FAR), and Regulation (REG).

Auditing and Attestation (AUD)

- Ethics, professional responsibilities, and general principles
- Assessing risk and developing a planned response
- Performing further procedures and obtaining evidence
- Forming conclusions and reporting

Time allotted: 4 hours

Format: Two multiple-choice tests, three task-based simulation tests

Business Environment and Concepts (BEC)

- Corporate governance

- Economic concepts and analysis
- Financial management
- Information technology
- Operations management

Time allotted: 4 hours

Format: Two multiple-choice tests, two task-based simulation tests, and one written communication test

Financial Accounting and Reporting (FAR)

- Conceptual framework, standard-setting, and financial reporting
- Select financial statement accounts
- Select transactions
- State and local governments

Time allotted: 4 hours

Format: Two multiple-choice tests, three task-based simulation tests

Regulation (REG)

- Ethics, professional responsibilities, and federal tax procedures
- Business law
- Federal taxation of property transactions
- Federal taxation of individuals
- Federal taxation of entities

Time allotted: 4 hours

Format: Two multiple-choice tests, three task-based simulation tests

While the CPA Exam is the same for all candidates, other requirements may differ by jurisdiction.

When applying for your license, verify that you have the required college credit hours. Generally, you must have 150 with a concentration in accounting. This includes 30 hours in accounting subjects and 24 hours in business administration subjects.

The rules vary by state, but the CPA usually requires at least two years of working under the supervision of a CPA. Getting the final sign-off can be very challenging for a management accountant who meets some but not all requirements.

What is the difference between a CMA & CPA?

The main difference between the CMA & CPA is the nature of their work.

CPAs work in public accounting, which are service firms that provide audit and tax services for their clients. Thus, the body of knowledge that makes up the CPA is focused entirely on these two disciplines.

The CMA focuses on preparing professionals to master all cost accounting concepts discussed in section 1. The exam teaches what is practical and current to thrive in this profession.

My Experience & Recommendation On The CMA & CPA

I began my career at DuPont, and the credential that everyone knew there was the CPA. So, following the crowd, I signed up for the CPA, studied, and passed each part successfully. However, the tricky part was the requirement to work under a CPA. My current supervisor didn't fit the bill, and luckily, I was assigned to another supervisor who was. It worked out for me.

However, several of my peers were not so lucky. They met the 150-credit requirement but didn't have the right supervisor. Despite several passing all four parts of the exam, they were stuck.

I'm sharing this story to illustrate how cumbersome the CPA has become to achieve. Even more, the CPA exam has transformed over time and, in the future, will no longer cover any part of cost accounting as it has traditionally done.

If you pursue a career in management accounting, the CMA makes much more sense than the CPA, which teaches students auditing/tax laws.

The CMA program was designed to meet the evolving needs of

the business by focusing on skills such as strategic thinking, financial analysis, and the ability to convert data into dialogue.

The CMA (Certified Management Accountant) program is a valuable investment for those looking to challenge themselves and succeed in the ever-changing world of finance. The certification will equip you with analytical skills, problem-solving abilities, and other vital competencies needed on your journey ahead. When faced with any challenges, they can come out ahead of the competition.

I have my MBA, CMA, and CPA and frequently advise students that the CMA has been the most useful to me.

What Credential Should You Pursue?

Depending on your career plans, it may be worth it to become both a Certified Public Accountant (CPA) and a Certified Management Accountant (CMA). Not only are dual CPAs and CMAs more valuable due to their broad scope of knowledge, but they command higher salaries.

While many CPAs choose to practice in public accounting, many follow career paths outside of public in corporate accounting, government, academia, and the non-profit sector.

A significant benefit of continuing your accounting education is that you can enhance and develop the skills you've already utilized in the workplace; both the CPA and CMA can increase your depth of accounting subject matter knowledge.

However, there are some critical distinctions between the two. For example, after you pass your CPA Exam, you must also become licensed, which is done at a state level.

On the other hand, the CMA requires membership in the IMA (Institute of Management Accountants). Whereas the "what" focus of the CPA involves more accounting-specific training, the "why" focus of the CMA deals more with financial accounting and asset and performance management. Despite the differences, there are many ways that both credentials overlap and complement each other.

CMA training can open new doors to CPAs aspiring to build careers outside the traditional public firm path in cost and management. CPAs who become CMAs may find a job as financial analysts, budget analysts, cost accountants, controllers, etc.

The CMA, essentially, is valuable to CPAs who want to transition out of public accounting. There is less value in a CMA earning a CPA afterward.

How Long Should You Study For The CMA Exam?

If you decide to pursue the CMA, it helps to understand how much time to budget to complete the exams. When you register with the IMA and join the certificate program, the clock starts running for taking both parts of the exam. You have 12 months to take the exam, and you must complete the CMA program within three years.

The IMA recommends that candidates study for 150 to 170 hours per exam, and there are two exam parts. Each part is a four-hour test that includes 100 multiple-choice questions and two essay questions.

Assess your strengths and weaknesses in preparation. If you did well in a recent cost management class, you might be able to spend less time on that topic. Other exam concepts, however, may be more challenging for you.

Misconceptions

A common misconception is that the CPA is the right choice for students to pursue because it is more well-known.

While the CPA generally has more popularity, the CMA continues to rise as a world-renowned credential while the CPA has decreased drastically.

Following recent structural changes to the CPA exam, the number of candidates and newly licensed CPAs in 2018 fell to the lowest level in 10 years. The number of CPA candidates fell 7% to 36,827, and the number of newly licensed CPAs dropped 6% to 23,941.

For the fiscal year ended June 30, 2019, ICMA® (Institute of Certified Management Accountants) welcomed a record-high 11,530 new CMAs, up an impressive 89% compared to last year. For the same period, new candidates joining the CMA program totaled 49,862, increasing 26% compared to last year.

Conclusion

Having an accounting credential behind your name means a lot in the working world.

If you have any doubt, go to any career site and perform a job search for CMAs and CPAs to determine the demand and types of jobs that each qualifies for. Credentials prove to hiring managers that you know your stuff and are passionate about your work.

While the CMA is the preferred option for management accountants, the CPA should also be assessed and compared.

Once you have one credential, you can continue adding others and becoming more distinguished. Over time, this will allow you to stand far apart from the crowd and help you earn the salary and recognition you deserve.

Wrap-Up

After reading through these actionable ways to prepare for a career in management accounting, you are well on your way.

A great resume isn't built overnight and can't be done on graduation, so identify the steps you wish to take, put a plan together, and then commit to achieving it.

Getting started early is a smart way to learn more about your career options and give yourself an early advantage so that when it's time to find a job, you're the top pick for multiple employers.

Complete your degree, learn the necessary skills, take advantage of your school's resources, join the IMA, begin studying for your CMA credential, and you'll be well on your way to achieving your dreams.

PART 3: GROWING IN YOUR EARLY CAREER

"Be the Change You Want to See"

After getting hired into your first management accounting job, the first few years (1-5 yrs) are an exciting time of hyper-growth for young professionals.

This is often the first time you will experience living independently, earning an income, and paying bills. Over the next handful of years, you will grow personally and professionally by leaps and bounds.

These early years are incredibly formative to long-term success for several reasons.

Your initial working years are an excellent opportunity to learn and identify your strengths/weaknesses and career preferences. There is also more leeway here to make mistakes and adjustments.

The first years are crucial to establishing good habits and building a solid career foundation. The on-the-job experience exposes new hires to real-world scenarios and allows them to sharpen technical and soft skills.

By developing your ability to apply the business and financial concepts you learned in school, young professionals can begin to have an impact and demonstrate their value to their employer and industry.

This chapter will cover the following topics:

1. Developing Industry Awareness
2. General Career Advice- Developing a Value-Creation Mindset
3. Establishing Relationships
4. Developing and Enhancing Your Technical Skills
5. Developing Your Communication Skills
6. Getting Promoted
7. Career Transitions

1. Developing Industry Awareness

Before covering any other topic, it is well worth discussing the management career path and the trends that define the role of today and the future. You will learn about the state of the finance function and the new expectations for finance professionals.

The Role Of Finance

Finance disciplines are amidst a transformation brought on by new technologies and Covid-19. Many initiatives that were stuck and struggled to gain support now have the full attention of executives.

Organizations have a fresh understanding of the importance of having a future-oriented and robust accounting and planning function to incorporate multiple scenarios and support better decision-making.

Better technology will help finance handle uncertainty and execute its value proposition as real-time information and auto-generated analysis move closer to reality.

Finance now focuses on serving stakeholders through analytics and business insights, which mandate new capabilities. Finance is shifting some legacy responsibilities to other functions, centers of excellence, and outsourced partners to bolster its capabilities.

Controllership is standardizing tasks and processes and bringing online end-to-end process automation. Historical and time-delayed reporting is shifting to provide multi-dimensional, integrated, real-time insights.

The silos between Controllership and financial planning and analysis (FP&A) functions are also delineating, providing the opportunity for integration and collaboration to realize the tangible value and contribute to the larger business strategy.

The finance professional's role must adapt to keep up with the times and business needs. New skill sets, perspectives, and knowledge are required. As a young professional, you will be critical in playing a role in building tomorrow's finance function.

Automation

Finance will continue to automate processes to provide real-time and meaningful financial insights. Automation targets are expanding from end-to-end processes affecting multiple business areas rather than siloed activities.

Pockets of innovation are gaining influence and the support and funding they need to build new capabilities across an organization. With automation in place, finance can progress to next-level analytics consisting of big data, AI analytics, and predictive modeling to inform business strategy and decisions.

Automation has progressed slowly over the years, led by market leaders, but today, mid and small-market players are accelerating to close the gap. A traditional lack of standardized processes and investment in data architecture slowed automation and shifted focus to the cloud.

Automation has had mixed results in the past, with the automation of mostly task-based activities requiring scale to achieve a return on investment. Instead, the growth of enterprise resource planning (ERP) capabilities highlights cloud ERP's more critical role in driving automation across end-to-end processes.

Finance Cycles

Historically, management accountants have been involved with closing the books each month, quarter, and year and then producing static analysis at a historical point in time.

This type of reporting is not acceptable anymore.

Although real-time financial analysis isn't yet available, quarterly reporting will gradually lose relevance for investors and management, who require more timely information to make decisions.

Finance will be expected to remain agile, with the ability to post results between external reporting cycles while also meeting evolving internal management needs.

For management accountants, the change in expectations around finance cycles means two things. First, automation will shorten closing cycles, and reporting cadences will accelerate.

Rather than waiting until month-end to report KPIs (key performance indicators) and operational/financial metrics, management accountants must design processes and tools that provide daily, weekly, and monthly analysis in a self-service environment. Instead of printing reports, business users will be trained to access analytical tools and ask and then answer their own questions.

Controllership will focus less on reducing close cycles and more on real-time information and continuous accounting with less value placed on historical reporting.

The challenge will be breaking the monthly reporting cycle and moving toward a more agile accounting model. However, real-time visibility into performance and projections remains aspirational. Since the platforms, data foundation, and finance routines aren't yet there to support it; the near-term focus will be less about immediate results and more about forecasts and analytics that inform commercial decisions.

Operating Models

Cost reduction has historically been the driver of changes to finance operating models. But that focus will evolve and expand finance's core capabilities and define what it can deliver in partnership with other functions.

Remote work will likely remain to some degree, and many finance organizations will be set up to accommodate it. The early days of the Covid-19 pandemic emphasized the benefits of a distributed finance workforce equipped with collaboration tools around clearly defined work processes.

New service delivery models will also expand Controllership's core capabilities and value in partnership with other functions. As the overall business prizes, new capabilities, and coordination with partner networks expand, the traditional silos between functions will dissolve as they absorb responsibilities historically managed elsewhere.

ERP Systems

Through acquisitions and functional enhancements, ERP vendors have primarily staved off competition from smaller and more innovative competitors to maintain the status quo with their legacy products. Big players will continue to swallow up competitors but are now more open to expanding their offering and providing new cutting-edge capabilities to grow market share as one-stop providers. In addition, on-premises servers and support are disappearing as ERPs increasingly move to the cloud.

Cloud-based solutions offer continuous technological improvements that streamline processes and automate activities across all financial processes. As specialized apps and microservices have grown more sophisticated, ERP providers have also upped their game by rapidly adding new features and making acquisitions.

These specialized vendors and cloud-based ERPs play a critical role in Finance and Controllership's continued digital transformation from here on out, moving from back-office cost centers to the front-office drivers of business value.

Data

Standardized, high-quality data will become even more essential, as data is the foundation for business insights, automation, and touchless operations. Finance will double down on massive data cleanup efforts to ensure data integrity and set the right governance strategy.

Data will provide the foundation for any successful finance organization moving forward.

Controllership relies heavily on data for strategic insights, enhanced analytics, and more driver-based reporting frameworks, making data quality crucial to the function's performance. Many professionals face challenges compiling relevant, understandable, and effective data. Data's ever-increasing volume and complexities only intensify these hurdles.

Management accountants will play a leading role here by developing business acumen and assuming leadership roles to oversee enterprise data strategy, systems frameworks, and processes to meet the challenge and critical need to generate impactful data and reporting frameworks.

Finance And Data

Historically, companies have hired and relied on IT and scientists to maintain data integrity and systems. But, due to siloing, there has been a painful disconnect between operations and business needs and IT plans and resources.

Organizations will still utilize data scientists as we advance, but they will increasingly collaborate on data integration and analysis with Finance. Finance, on their side, is becoming much more data and systems literate to articulate business needs and test/develop solutions.

Finance professionals are needed to configure and customize digital tools to generate insights while more of the workforce operates remotely as hybrid work models become common.

While traditional finance skills remain central to the function, those with business acumen, a service mindset, and digital savvy will be in greatest demand.

Reporting

Historical financial reporting and inflexible budgeting and forecasting processes can no longer support effective decision-making in the current uncertain environment, where the speed of change is ever-increasing.

Much time in reporting has generally been spent extracting and manipulating data, with only a tiny fraction spent on analysis. Modern ETL (Extract, Transform, Load) tools like PowerQuery and PowerBI completely shift the dynamic. The systems now automate what has manually been done, and much more time and effort is spent on generating meaningful commentary and analysis.

While those currently leading finance functions remain uneasy about using self-service data, the path forward is clear. Getting comfortable with self-service will be accomplished by putting more data-savvy finance professionals into management accounting roles.

Self-service applications will become more familiar with the right financial resources in place. Finance will spend more time working with the business to harmonize discrepancies between self-service tools, language processing, and record systems.

Dynamic reporting tools and processes will help finance move past static reports, providing more interactive tools and drill-down functionality analysis. This can deliver relevant and effective analytics at the businesses' fingertips to generate valuable data-driven insights, immediate answers, and more agile decision-making.

Predictive forecasting models incorporating real-time data, automation, and predictive analytics can hotwire traditional planning with a more agile process of accessing potential scenarios, analyzing risks, and enhancing insights for more informed decision-making.

Wrap-Up

As you have just read, today's finance career and function drastically differ from a generation ago. New skills and talent are critical to bridging the technological divide and giving businesses the insights and tools to succeed.

Management accountants have a central role in each evolution, leading to more exciting work and more impactful and rewarding careers.

2. Create Value

The following section will review general career advice for the modern management accountant. Too often, accountants have been relegated to siloed functions and dark corners of the office. However, the modern professional must have a different outlook and impact on the organization.

Be Curious

Being curious should be a central attitude you carry throughout your career. Management accountants are expected to understand the business, establish relationships, and understand how things work today and how they should work tomorrow. You can't do this if you are not curious and have an open mind.

Strive to ask questions and learn as much as you can every day. By doing this, you can excel in your career and stay interested and exciting (to peers, your boss, your future employer, whatever the case may be).

A famous phrase goes, "When we stop learning, we stop growing," which happens to be very accurate and practical.

When we stop learning, we also stop caring as much. The world and finance are changing around you daily, and there is always something new to learn to keep you engaged.

Manage Your Career

Plan to manage your career. Although your first employer may promise to develop and look out for you, only you know what is best for yourself.

Don't assume others will possess the same ambition and perspectives you do. To achieve your career plan, you must advocate for yourself and speak up to have your voice heard.

You won't be able to get everywhere on your own, so identifying and bringing in mentors and advisors for guidance is also key to supporting your career aspirations.

Understand what you want, why you want it, and what it will take to achieve your plan.

Another word of advice is never to become too comfortable. Once improvements are rolled out and learning opportunities dry up, initiate discussions to see what else you can gain exposure to. If these discussions don't lead anywhere internally, beginning to look externally is an intelligent move.

Think Like An Entrepreneur

You are the business of you.

If you learn to think like an entrepreneur, you'll think and work more effectively. You are responsible for investing in your own skills, growth, integrity, reputation, and brand.

Like a business, you need a career strategy, and you need to become really good at executing that strategy. Determine what makes you unique, valuable, and marketable, and press the pedal on those attributes.

If you neglect any aspect of your career, you can't expect your paycheck and title to keep rising.

Don't Be Complacent

Accountants typically get a bad rap as "box-checkers" and "bean-counters." There is an outdated notion that management accountants follow the rules, do as their told, and complete basic tasks.

There is some truth to this, considering how the role has progressed over time, but this is very far from the truth today. Today, accountants are expected and rewarded for challenging bad practices, poor processes, and dogma that detract from performance.

Regularly question your profession's and industry's orthodoxies. Ask why not and press for answers. Don't settle for "because" or, even worse, "we've always done it that way."

It becomes easy for many to settle into a job and become complacent. As a new hire in an existing organization, you can identify many people like this who have become blind to operational deficiencies. Your fresh eyes are valuable for questioning "what could be," not accepting "what is."

For those bold enough, challenging the status quo is a great way to build your reputation and take leadership in improving the business.

Don't Get Put In A Box

It is common for professionals to get mischaracterized and miss many promising career opportunities. In management accounting, it used to be that finance professionals would close the book and issue reports. They stayed in their lane. They weren't asked about process improvements, data, or systems.

Don't let that happen to you.

Be dynamic and valuable in different ways. Find something about your career that intrigues you, even if it isn't the 'sexy' issue. Discover what you are good at regarding the nature of the work, and then find a way to marry those two things. Don't get put into a box – advocate for yourself to ensure you can succeed.

Also, don't put yourself in a box and limit your potential. Think broadly about your role within the business. Be curious to learn as much as you can about the company and industry to strengthen your relevance. The combination of deep technical skillsets and deep industry knowledge, and technology awareness will position you as an indispensable resource to stakeholders as you develop relationships.

Never stop pursuing differentiation. What you learned in school will be archaic in years; it is a constant evolution, and you must stay ahead, so you don't get left behind.

Understand How Your Firm Makes Money

As a management accountant, it is easy to get stuck in a rut and only know costing information. Sure, this is valuable, but this limits your growth.

Spend plenty of time in your early career interacting and talking with different departments to learn what they do and understand how they all connect and interact with finance.

Understanding how your firm generates profits will make your presence more valuable and increase your involvement in more initiatives. Demonstrate your interest and indicate you want to help perpetuate the firm.

Performing High-Quality Work

Whatever you do, strive for excellence. Whenever you start a new role, you are likely taking over what someone else used to do.

Find ways to optimize, improve, and automate your tasks to improve their accuracy, completeness, and timing.

Then, reach out and ask for more challenging assignments- This will go a far way to demonstrating your interest and initiative.

When you work, strive not to complete work as fast as possible, but take the time you need to ensure your work is high-quality, error-free, and complete. Too often, young professionals think speed is the name of the game, and errors occur.

Once you make a few errors, trust begins to erode, and as you know, trust takes a long time to rebuild.

Learn Critical Thinking Skills

While technical skills are essential, critical-thinking skills are just as, if not more important. Critical thinking skills help young professionals anticipate environmental changes and adjust to the evolving needs of the business. The most successful accountants will analyze key business drivers such as financial and operational data, regulatory requirements, technology changes, and risks and compile these individual elements into a strategic approach that helps their organization evolve.

Cultivate Curiosity- Ask "Stupid" Questions

This section's final advice is to take advantage of your newbie status in your first role. Being new gives you a rare opportunity to ask lots of questions without feeling awkward or silly. Even if you think you know the answer, ask the question again to confirm your suspicions.

In this ever-changing, fast-paced world, power lies in letting go of the need to have all the answers and opening yourself up to possibilities. Instead of aiming for the perfect solutions, learn to ask great questions (not only of others but of yourself, too!).

Asking lots of questions will indicate to those around you that you are curious and want to learn. You will also be able to establish many relationships that will be crucial over time.

Wrap-Up

As you can tell, working as a management accountant today holds much promise and potential. Instead of doing what has always been done, new professionals are the fresh energy required to help organizations advance into the future. Your career growth will improve if you keep learning, demonstrate interest, and find unique ways to add value.

3. Establishing Relationships

As previously mentioned, building, maintaining, and strengthening relationships with business stakeholders is essential for management accountants.

To obtain the information and insights, not in the general ledger, you need to interact with people and get them to like and trust you.

To truly be different and add value from a client's point of view, you must be good at the stuff that is relationship-based, not just technical-based. The ability to advise, show empathy and relate to others on a human level will be the critical skills we need to develop in our people.

A managerial accountant will interact more with the other departments than other accountants. Management accountants must work side-by-side with various departments to determine where improvements are needed.

Look around and get to know as many people as you can. Success in your career comes from the relationships you build- No one does it alone.

Managers

The relationship with your manager is an important one. Done right, your manager will trust you and be your most prominent advocate. Done wrong, they'll be the first to kick you out the door.

The key is to establish expectations and discuss what success looks like at different milestones with managers. Begin managing expectations via consistent communication. Each day, share a quick list of tasks you're working on to ensure alignment. As you have questions or challenges with the work, understand the best time and method to discuss them.

To stay on your boss's good side, the best thing you can do is follow through on your commitments and keep them in the loop. No one wants to be blindsided with unexpected news they should know, nor do they want to micromanage you and constantly remind you to do the agreed-upon work.

If it's helpful, set up regular status meetings with your manager once a week to discuss what:

a) You've accomplished,
b) You're working on that's on schedule,
c) You're working on that's not on schedule (and how to fix it), and
d) Is on hold due to other priorities and constraints.

Be open and honest with your manager, and they'll gladly be your coach, mentor, and biggest cheerleader.

Coworkers

Get to know your coworkers. Understand what tasks they perform, the purpose of their role, and how their position fits into the overall finance function or business.

It also helps to make an extra effort and get to know at least some of them personally. Remembering coworkers' names helps to improve your likeability and reputation.

"Hey, you!" only gets you so far.

Industry Groups & Professional Associations

Industry groups and professional associations are a great forum to meet others who work in the industry and have roles similar to yours. By joining and becoming active in industry groups, you will establish relationships that can lead to future opportunities and help you benchmark how your organization faces particular challenges.

Industry groups hold events throughout the year and expose you to various backgrounds and perspectives from which you can learn and benefit.

The Importance Of Networking

The word networking causes many young professionals to cringe, and honestly, most people rather be anywhere else than at a businessy event where they know very few people.

These sorts of social interactions are not natural and take some getting used to, but are a worthwhile pursuit.

Sign up, go, and stick with them. Learn how to make the most of networking experiences. Go with a plan in mind or certain professionals to speak with. In time, networking events can be helpful to find new friends, find mentors, learn new ideas, and become familiar with industry leaders

Seek Out Potential Mentors

Finding a mentor early in your career should be high on your career agenda. Mentors are people with more experience in similar career paths or industries who make time to get to know you and provide feedback, ideas, and guidance to questions and challenges when you're unsure who to turn to.

Look for more experienced colleagues with who you feel a connection and who can coach you towards success. A mentor with more experience can help you identify common career missteps and pitfalls that they or others have experienced.

Throughout a career, you will likely have different mentors for different reasons, which is ok- Just be upfront with expectations and needs.

Helping Others

One of the best ways to establish relationships is to go out of your way to help colleagues solve their problems. If you spend time with others and learn about their challenges, think of unique solutions, and then discuss improvements, your relationships will soar.

You can offer to help others during their crunch time with projects, but only after checking with your supervisor and ensuring there isn't anything else they would prefer you were doing.

A management accountant's intimacy with data, automation, and reporting tools will benefit colleagues with less awareness or resources to improve their workflows and help them spend more time on value-added tasks.

Seek & Provide Feedback

Seeking and providing feedback and establishing mutual relationships where both parties can share a second perspective of each other's work effectiveness can be a highly valuable exercise.

Often, we have a narrative in our minds we tell ourselves about how work is going. We may think we are on track and doing very well, but it is wise always to find others to weigh in and assess what you are doing and how you are doing it.

Balanced feedback from multiple viewpoints is the best way to assess performance and identify improvement opportunities.

Offering to share feedback with others on how they are perceived is also valuable and usually welcomed. Establishing several mutual feedback relationships will strengthen your likability and help you avoid awkward misconceptions about how good you really are (or not).

Wrap-Up

To be a management accountant with strong technical skills but lackluster relationship skills is a recipe for disaster.

Management accountants are no longer isolated number-counters but have evolved into strategic business partners. To be an effective business partner, you need to form strong relationships that give you the real pulse of the organization.

Your job, essentially, is to be "in the know" and have both the numbers and stories behind everything that is going on in the business. To thrive as a management accountant, prioritize building relationships and technical skills simultaneously.

A management accountant with better relationships over technical skills beats the skilled accountant with no friends every time.

4. Technical Skills

Technical skills are how work gets done. As you've read in earlier sections, management accounting today requires highly skilled professionals capable of adapting to new technologies while mastering the accounting basics.

Establishing a plan to identify and develop the skills you need through on-the-job experience, courses, and working with others is key to staying on track and staying competitive in the field.

The exciting aspect of management accounting today is that there are many opportunities to differentiate yourself and stand apart from anyone else in the organization. If you can identify skills in need, build your knowledge, and demonstrate leadership in leading teams and building solutions, your career will thrive for years to come.

As management accounting is transitioning, many organizations are not where they need to be regarding technologies or skilled professionals. If you strive to become highly skilled, you will increase your reputation and earnings potential in your firm and future.

Devise A Professional Development Plan

Step one is to develop a professional development plan. Once you have experience on the job after several weeks or months, you should have a good feel for the required and in-demand skillsets.

Discussing what you are seeing and experiencing with your manager and colleagues is wise to confirm your perceptions. Consult managers, the Human Resources department, and professionals in your field and determine what certifications, coursework, and/or degrees are advisable to advance your career.

Once you have a consensus around where you need to develop skill-wise, put together a plan to turn your aspirations into reality.

Make your plan SMART (specific, measurable, actionable,

realistic, and timely). Define milestones of what you will learn by when and share your plan with others to keep yourself accountable. Set clear goals and objectives regarding what you will learn and acquire skills.

Learn To Learn

Learning itself is a skill that takes time to master. Professional life is much different from college, where information is quickly learned, tested, and forgotten.

In your career, you will need to remember what you have learned and continuously build on your accounting foundation. Reflect within yourself to identify the patterns that produce the best study results.

Blocking out time and avoiding distractions is a great way to go. Remember that you will have to make short-term sacrifices for a long-term benefit.

Make a serious effort to buy your study materials and let your friends and family know that you are fully committed to mastering your trade. The longer you wait, the harder it is to get back into the groove of constantly studying.

Read to Lead

33% of high school graduates never read another book for the rest of their lives, and 42% of college grads never read another book after college.

Shocking but true. Do not let this same trend happen to you.

Aside from learning technical skills, being a management accountant involves having general business knowledge. You should understand business best practices, trends, and significant events and articulate opinions on these matters.

Focusing your career solely on accounting knowledge will limit your growth and potential. Make reading a habit and read from a variety of sources.

Books, journals, HBR (Harvard Business Reviews), and WSJ (Wall Street Journal) are excellent choices.

Enrich One Another

Co-workers are a great source of learning for a young professional. As you build relationships, take note of what your colleagues can do better than you and ask if it would be ok to learn from them.

99% of the time, colleagues are flattered that you are interested. Shadow them and learn what they do, how they do it, and why. Often, colleagues have a lot more experience and work in a certain way for specific reasons. Understand their methodologies and rationale to accelerate your learning.

It is also wise to take the initiative to learn about your co-workers' roles and the work done by their department. You will make internal moves by scouting interesting departments should the need or opportunity arises over time.

Professional Certification Programs

In part 2 of this book, we discussed the CMA certification.

It is a fantastic source of training and technical knowledge. While you are young in your career and do not have family commitments, take advantage of this time to commit to earning your CMA and then exploring other valuable credentials.

The CMA is the most valuable and will pay significant dividends throughout your career.

Most Training Is Useless

"It is, after all, the dab of grit that seeps into an oyster's shell that makes a pearl, not pearl-making seminars with other oysters."

-Stephen King

"Businesses often use training as a surrogate for the hard work of true skill development."

-Bill Peper, facilitator within General Motors' Standards for Excellence process

"Training is too often used as an inexpensive way to look like you're doing something if you're a manager. As typically

done, it requires little time and little personal change."

-Ted Harro

By far, the most effective approach to learning new skills as individuals is to apply deliberate practice to training and develop grit to set, reach, and reset our goals to improve as we progress in our careers.

Yes, we can improve ourselves and encourage others to learn independently, but organized group education is another animal.

When learning involves more than an individual effort and takes place in a corporate setting, we take something fulfilling and valuable, squeeze the life out of it, and transform it into this unholy abomination we call "training."

When most people hear the word training today, the blood runs out of their faces, and their body slumps as if life has just been sucker-punched. Training connotes an experience that is a painful, time-consuming, and utterly useless exercise by most accounts, pretending to take employee development seriously.

For whatever reason, as soon as more than one person is added to an educational exercise, all the rules and best practices go right out the window. Not only is most training in today's companies ineffective, but the purpose, timing, and content of training are flawed by design.

We've all been through the gamut of training workshops, online courses, and lectures that give training a bad name. Most training has become a box-checking exercise rather than a genuine development activity.

Only a tiny fraction of formal training is ever put into practice, and as a result, most business training is a waste of money and time for everyone involved.

Because most training, courses, and conferences are organized as stand-alone events, they are deemed irrelevant because they are disconnected from the work done and the problems at hand.

While we attend organized training sessions as a prerequisite to keeping our jobs, many of us have developed our own tips and tricks to get through the sessions as quickly as possible. We'll patiently listen and half-tune out the instructors, then go through the motions to complete the courses and guess our way through any sort of assessment at the end. Once we see a window of opportunity to escape, we'll quickly run back to our offices to finally get back to doing our jobs.

Year after year, it's the same charade we torture ourselves and the other people we work with. “Frustrating and ineffective” describe the situation lightly.

More than anecdotal evidence or perceptions, there's a great HBR article titled, "Where Companies Go Wrong with Learning and Development," which brings to light the hard evidence of the training plight:

1. "75% of 1,500 managers surveyed from across 50 organizations were dissatisfied with their company's Learning & Development (L&D) function;
2. 70% of employees report that they don't have mastery of the skills needed to do their jobs;
3. Only 12% of employees apply new skills learned in L&D programs to their jobs; and
4. Only 25% of respondents to a recent McKinsey survey believe that training measurably improved performance. "

The source of the training problem has been cited on all sorts of issues, whether lack of managerial clarity, uninterested learners, or outdated training practices.

Suppose you've had experience attending corporate training. In that case, you will have noticed that most training is designed from a top-down hierarchy and is initiated by someone at the executive or director level who thinks: "The people need these skills, and we'll hire someone to teach it to them."

The people who perform the training are so detached from the organization that they don't know how to connect the message to its priorities or the work done each day. Or, if the course is video-based, the training is so generic that the message tries to reach everyone but, in doing so, reaches no one.

Rarely has someone come back from a three-hour marathon workshop and immediately applied what they have just half-listened to. Knowledge decay occurs quickly when employees don't use the skills they've learned after training.

To illustrate this point, German psychologist Hermann Ebbinghaus pioneered experimental studies of memory in the late 19th Century, culminating with his discovery of "The Forgetting Curve." He found that if new information isn't applied, we'll forget about 75% of it after just six days. New skills must be practiced and applied.

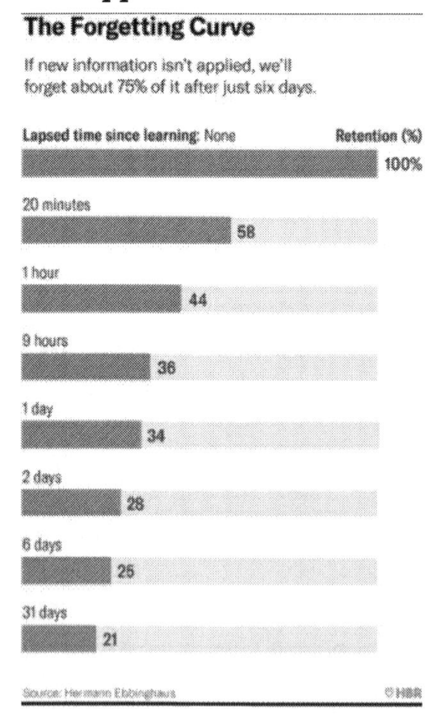

If we were to step back, reflect, and think about the skills we have learned throughout our lives and careers, we would find that the most impactful learning occurs when facing an immediate and pressing problem. An obstacle that halts progress causes us to apply all of our focus and energy to conduct our research, test the idea, and apply it.

The root cause of the core problem with training — that training is rarely applied — comes from training designed and dictated by people other than those who do the work.

Like most other practices, the best training is most helpful when it comes from a decentralized process. When someone comes across an idea, a tool, or technology that helps them do their job with more significant results in less time, they should be so excited that they can't wait to share that information with others.

Even though someone may not be a professional trainer, what matters is what is being shared and whether or not it can be applied to real business problems. Training done by an organization's people results in much higher acceptance and application rates. Bossidy commented in Execution, "80% of learning should occur outside the classroom. Every leader and supervisor needs to be a teacher; classroom learning should be about giving them the tools they need."

To maximize the training's effectiveness:

1. The training should be conducted by the teams and groups that work together regularly to enact the training and establish collective commitments.
2. If the training applies to what the team is working on, good ideas and practices can be discussed in detail and then tested. A team member would share the information they discovered and the application and gauge interest to see if others would like to solve similar problems.
3. Then, real training would occur—no fancy PowerPoints or speeches but real issues and real solutions in real-time.

When people understand and "own" the importance of a topic, they recognize its purpose, meaning, value, and role in their careers; thus, they often seek out and find resources. Any person who has found a good idea and has applied it to their work should be a trainer for others.

Rather than adding distractions to other people's busy schedules, training should be structured and carried out in a way that helps others improve the quality or efficiency of what they are doing today. Training should be scheduled on topics that can be applied straightaway.

The key is to assess the effectiveness of training offered in your organization by asking the following questions:

1. What behaviors must change to convince people that new skills, abilities, and capabilities are required?
2. Are the right people performing the training?
3. How will the impact of the training be measured? Who will perform the follow-ups?
4. What must happen before and after the training sessions occur to bring about change?

Today's dynamic business environment calls for organizations and their people to adapt to changing circumstances and always be learning rapidly.

Excellent training requires allowing people closest to the work to experience new ideas, discuss them, test them, and implement them. With the proper preparation and follow-up, training can be compelling. And even better, decentralized training can be organized and executed in much less time and cost less than the traditional methodology.

Furthermore, as technology continues to grow and organizations face new challenges at a furious pace of change, we must arm ourselves with the information necessary to adapt to our circumstances. What may have worked or used to work to solve a particular problem may no longer be applicable.

We must commit to becoming the best versions of ourselves to set ourselves up for sustained success. Without all this in mind, training will be (and usually is) a wasted opportunity.

Never Stop Learning

Earning a college degree doesn't mean you get to retire the thinking cap. Knowledge is a lifelong pursuit that, in itself, becomes meaningful. As we expand our knowledge, we grow and expand our thinking of what is possible.

Be prepared for a transition period as you meet new colleagues, learn new computer systems, and acclimate to a full-time, entirely professional world. Take advantage of this early period and embrace as much as possible and be a sponge the first year.

Just as the management accounting profession is evolving today, it will likely evolve again in the future. To ensure you are ready, you need to have your finger on the pulse to understand which skills are critical and the commitment to continue accumulating and demonstrating that knowledge.

Never. Stop. Learning.

If I could offer just two pieces of advice to you, it would be this:

1. Never stop learning, &
2. Completely master Microsoft Excel

5. Communication Skills

A crucial part of managerial accounting is presenting your analysis and conclusions to the management teams in your firm.

You will need to develop strong written and spoken communication skills. While developing strong technical skills and relationships are the foundation of management accounting, the next natural step is to share your knowledge and finding with others.

You must develop strong communication skills to communicate your messages, findings, and recommendations.

Soft Skills

Soft skills are those that deal with interacting with other people. Soft skills include holding a professional conversation, influencing, and selling ideas to others.

An accountant can be as technically capable as anyone, but if they are unable to communicate effectively with business stakeholders, think on their feet, juggle tasks, or come up with a solution to a client's complex problem, they will not have the same impact as a less technical, but more well-rounded peer.

Accountants are essential, active members of corporate teams, and as such, they must constantly interact and communicate with people. They no longer hold the unfortunate reputation of being relegated to the back office, perusing stacks of numbers beneath the harsh light of a desk lamp.

Soft skills involve interpersonal communication, time management, problem-solving, collaboration, creativity, and leadership aptitude.

Master Speaking Skills

As an accounting professional, you must convey complex information in terms that everyone can understand.

While technical skills are essential, verbal and written communication skills matter a lot to convey your knowledge to others. Many talented accountants who enter the workforce are very bright but struggle to carry a conversation or write a decent email. Even though the emphasis is on technology, analytics, etc., you still need strong communication skills to advance your career.

The first step is to familiarize yourself with the topic. Next, research your audience, including their purpose for participating in the discussion, concerns, time constraints, and attitudes. Then, tailor your speech as appropriate. The more prepared and knowledgeable you are about the participants, the more confident you'll be and the greater your message's impact.

Whether you speak with a colleague, manager, or executive, you must speak confidently and concisely to tie complicated accounting explanations into business operations.

Master Formal Presentation Skills

As management accountants are heavily involved with analysis and decision-making support, eventually, they will need to present their findings to organizational leaders.

Preparing for these events can be nerve-racking for younger professionals, but steps can be taken to ensure success. First, practice what you will present. Know the material inside and out.

Great accountants don't read from PowerPoint decks, word for word, but use them as a storytelling guide. Managerial accountants learn to understand what influences people and bring an emotional and factual component to the information they share and present.

If you aren't confident speaking in front of others, practice with friends or colleagues to get comfortable. Better yet, watch a few TED talks to see what the experts do to draw in and captivate their audiences. Becoming a master public speaker takes time, but studying the craft and practicing goes far.

Master Active-Listening Skills

Management accountants will spend much time with others

to understand their contribution and assess performance. A fantastic skill to learn is active-listening to make the most of these interactions.

The more you genuinely listen to others, the more you can provide a valuable service and build lasting relationships. Take time to ask questions of others and give them the time they need to explain what they do and why they do it thoroughly.

Active listening means taking notes, using verbal cues to indicate attentiveness, and showing interest in the listener. Asking follow-up and clarifying questions show that you are interested and value the other person's time and efforts.

Giving people the time and attention they deserve will make them more open to sharing information crucial to the business.

Master Writing Skills

Writing is one of the most under-appreciated skills in business for communication. Too often, professionals get consumed with trying to keep up with their workload and fall victim to the tendency to become sloppy, inefficient, or ineffective with their writing.

Emails go unanswered, responses are full of spelling and grammatical errors, and the confusion around and issue only increases as either too many or too few people are included in responses.

A good management accountant will study the characteristics of good writing and strive to make their communication clear and crisp. Good written communication involves responding promptly, using tools to check spelling/grammar errors, and ensuring the right people are communicating.

It is always a bright idea to have a second party like a trusted peer or manager read over an email before sending it out to obtain feedback. Sending out hastily written and sloppy communication poorly reflects a young person's professionalism and character.

WRAP-UP

Communication is an essential part of management accounting. We can only obtain the real story of what is going on in the business and why by working with others. Management accountants can add significant value to their organizations when involved with financial figures and pairing them with these narratives.

Communication skills take time to master and are built around good habits. Study good communication and strive for excellence to bolster your career.

6. Getting Promoted

Getting promoted is an aspiration for all professionals. Earning a promotion means increasing your pay, receiving a more prestigious title, and earning the respect of your peers and colleagues.

Promotions tell the world that your contributions to the organization:

1. Are valued, and
2. You should be rewarded for your efforts, and
3. Elevated to a higher role to amplify your effect.

However, understanding who gets promoted, why, and when remains an ambiguous question to many young professionals. The section below will explain the key elements that drive promotions.

Become the Trusted Expert

Notice that the title does not say to be trusted or to be an expert; rather, to be the trusted expert. Setting yourself up for promotion involves a ton of work on the back-end to get good at what you do and demonstrate your knowledge and expertise by helping others solve shared business challenges.

Management accountants should be the trusted source for reporting, decision-making, and operational effectiveness. You will know that you have become the trusted expert when you are invited to most, if not all, important management meetings and are consulted to provide essential information and insights.

Being the trusted expert demonstrates your value, contribution, and influence in your organization. If you have expertise but are seldom consulted, find ways to make yourself and your work known to others.

Grow and Show Curiosity

As you've learned throughout this book, growing professionally and personally is part of the job as a management accountant.

Earning a promotion will be much more challenging if you are not growing, learning, and developing new skills, capabilities, or knowledge.

If you intend to get promoted, you should work with your organization to understand the knowledge gaps and then step up to learn and apply that knowledge.

Set goals with a challenging yet realistic timeline to complete different milestones. At the end of this time, compare your achievements with your goals to see how you've done.

Share your progress regularly with your manager to keep you accountable and see your capabilities and achievements. Showing growth and curiosity inside your role and the broader finance function and organization will tell the world you are promotion-ready.

Do Great Work

As management accountants are in crucial positions, their work and shared results must be accurate, timely, and complete. Your work should exceed expectations and lead to new requests from others. If your work contains errors and misses expectations, a promotion will not be in your near future.

Become the master of your domain, and then think about what you can do to demonstrate that you are already operating at a higher level and should be promoted accordingly.

Promotions are not given lightly, so just doing your work and hitting your targets isn't enough.

Think about it from your manager's point of view,

- Why would they promote you?
- Do you outperform peers and go above and beyond the norm?
- What do you do to "wow" the important people?

Become Known

The influence aspect of promotions has a notorious "yuck" factor for many professionals but is unavoidable for getting promoted.

The most talented person would be promoted in a perfect world, but the world doesn't work that way. Promotions are a combination of what you do, your potential, and also being liked. If decision-makers do not know or like you, they will advocate for something else.

Find ways to identify the formal and informal decision-makers in your organization and find ways to get on their radar and impress them. Build relationships and ensure they know the value they bring to the team.

Demonstrate Leadership

Many management accountants become very good at what they do but fail to see the importance of rising above the "me." Promotions are an indication that you are good at your job and have influence, both of which are aspects of leadership.

Leadership also involves saying what everyone is thinking but requires courage to say, taking the lead on projects, challenging convention, and defying the status quo. Leadership consists in rising above "me" to the "we," where you find ways to bring others on board for these efforts and initiatives. Being able to inspire others and lead them to action is what a leader does.

Even if you are not formally managing people yet, you must show you can be trusted to manage, develop and supervise the more junior staff or collaborate with peers in nearby roles.

Ask for the Promotion

To be promoted, you mu ask for it. It may sound weird, but you don't get it if you don't ask.

Communicate with your manager early on that being promoted to manager is what you want, and they will help you get there. Find ways to discuss how you are advancing on all the points mentioned above to show your growth and potential.

Quietly waiting to be rewarded for the efforts will only lead to frustration.

Make yourself and your goal known and ask for their advice on how to improve so that you can make your promotion a reality. If you need more guidance, consult your mentor, friends, and peers who have experience being promoted.

Be Patient

Even if you do everything right in preparing to be promoted, sometimes it just doesn't happen. For various reasons involving timing, influence, market factors, or restructuring, promotions could go to someone else, be delayed, or be unavailable on your timeline.

Be patient, to a degree. Generally, young professionals are promoted every 1.5-2.5 years. If a promotion hasn't happened for you, you can ask why and make your push more well known. If there are delays, you can usually learn more to understand the updated timeline and decide if that will work.

7. Career Progression & Promotions

Within the first few years of a professional's career, considering whether to stay at the current employer or go elsewhere will surely pop up. There are many different reasons why changing arrangements could or could not make sense.

As you read in the section above, you may have done everything right to become promotion-ready, but other factors have prevented or prevented your promotion. You have a choice to a. be more patient or b. go where you are more valued.

The key, like anything else, is to be mindful of the approach and avoid hasty and emotional decisions.

Building a great resume and career depend on making the right decisions to add value to organizations that make the most of your strengths and value you. The following steps will be covered in the section below to determine whether your current employer fits the bill or not and then decide what to do.

Make Your Employer Aware Of Concerns

One of the worst career mistakes is bottling your thoughts, feelings, and emotions inside. Every career has ups and downs, but if you don't have an outlet for these feelings, they can lead to poorly thought out outcomes.

Instead, the first step to take if you feel discontentment with your current employer is to have an honest discussion with your manager.

Explain your perspective, what you think is going right, wrong, and everything in between. Your manager will weigh in, add their thoughts, and either validate your feelings or offer a different viewpoint.

When things aren't going right, your manager can be a great resource to help change things up for the better or facilitate change. If additional help or guidance is needed, they will pitch in or find someone to guide you along.

Before you speak with your manager, though, it is wise to reflect on your thoughts and experiences, write them down, and talk them through with your spouse or close friends- This will help you hone in on issues or opportunities.

The worst-case scenario is that your manager tells you to keep pushing through and be patient with the circumstances, which isn't bad advice.

Consult With Others

When issues at work weigh on your mind, take time to process what is bugging you and find ways to articulate why these issues are occurring. Next, speak with family and close friends to provide a sounding board. Sometimes, minor problems can be smoothed over just by talking them through.

However, some issues are deeper rooted and may require further discussion or action at work. Speak with different people to obtain various perspectives and reflect on what has been said and why about your issues and challenges.

If all else fails, go for a few long walks to introspect and decide the path forward to pursue in the best interests of your career.

Explore Internal Options

Suppose you determine that a change is in order and have spoken with friends, family, and your manager. It is possible to make a career change within the organization to resolve the issue, keep you productive, and add value.

Sometimes this will involve swapping job responsibilities, changing departments, or job crafting where you get creative in adding more things you enjoy to counter the aspects you don't.

Your manager will likely want to keep you on board, so be open and honest with them.

Think Long-Term

Careers are very long, and each decision and career move on your resume matters. If you are unhappy, consider whether the issues can be solved with more time or if you need to change employers to maintain your mental and physical health.

If you must leave, consider what you have learned from a short-lived opportunity and identify what you will do differently in the future not to repeat it.

Even if you are unhappy in a role, try your best to keep up a positive attitude and keep up-to-date with your job responsibilities. Employers will gladly write a glowing letter of recommendation to help you get a different job if the situation isn't a good fit, but you are a great employee.

Perform Due Diligence For New Opportunities

Whether you are investigating new career opportunities because you have exceeded the growth potential in your current role or are dissatisfied, you must take your time and perform an appropriate level of diligence in finding your next career step.

Many young professionals often jump at another opportunity for a quick pay bump. But, in your early career, experiences matter more than small increments in pay. Look for opportunities with significant growth potential that fit your unique skill set and personality.

Before accepting a new job offer, perform a complete analysis of pay, bonus, and benefits to ensure that a new opportunity is as good as it seems. Also, check out sites like Glassdoor to see what others say about working there.

Don't Burn Bridges

Leaving a lousy job situation for greener grass might seem like an excellent opportunity to tell your current manager how you really feel. But, keep your emotions in check. If you do anything rash to tarnish your reputation, it can and will come back to bite you later in unexpected ways. Even if the job situation is draining, be professional, polite, and cordial when leaving.

Always:

1. Give at least two weeks' notice,
2. Document all work tasks, and
3. Leave the job better than you found it.

4. Thank your manager for the opportunity and wish them well.

Wrap-Up

Career transitions require care and diligence to assess whether a move is right for you and whether a move is the best option. By reflecting on your current opportunities and weighing the opinions of your friends, family, and manager, you can better determine if a job change is a smart move to make.

Sometimes a job change can open doors and accelerate growth, while other times, it can be a lateral move that impedes growth. The difference is having a balanced mindset and considering all factors when deciding to stay or go.

CONCLUSION- YOUR MODERN CAREER IN MANAGEMENT ACCOUNTING

After reading this book, you will be well-equipped to understand if a career in management accounting is right for you, prepare to get hired into your first management accounting job, and thrive in your early career years.

In my research of these topics, I was astonished to see that so little good information exists on the web, in books, or in articles. These are crucial topics that contain pertinent information for so many aspiring professionals.

I've enjoyed compiling this guide, sharing general wisdom, and tying in some of my personal experiences and intimate knowledge of this field and a management career. I am confident that the recent changes in management accounting make this career one of the brightest options today. It is where you can do work that matters, build influence, and get paid very well for doing so. Management accounting should be at the top of your list for those passionate about learning, growth, and pursuing a meaningful career.

Thank you for reading along- feel free to send any remaining questions or feedback to my email shared at the beginning of this book. In time, I will add them and any meaningful feedback.

Recommended Reading

I've read hundreds of books on business and leadership in my career. There are so many exciting and valuable perspectives that you can bring to work to enhance your contribution and accelerate your growth.

The list below contains my top 10 recommendations for young management accounting professionals:

1. *The Art of Action: How Leaders Close the Gaps between Plans, Actions, and Results* by Stephen Bungay
2. *Advice for a Successful Career in the Accounting Profession: How to Make Your Assets Greatly Exceed Your Liabilities* by Jerry Maginnis
3. *Getting Shit Done: The No-Nonsense Framework for Closing the Strategy-Execution Gap* by Benjamin Wann
4. *How to Win Friends & Influence People* by Dale Carnegie
5. *The 7 Habits of Highly Effective People: 30th Anniversary Edition* by Stephen R. Covey
6. *The SPEED of Trust: The One Thing that Changes Everything* by Stephen R. Covey
7. *So Good They Can't Ignore You: Why Skills Trump Passion in the Quest for Work You Love* by Cal Newport
8. *Grit: The Power of Passion and Perseverance* by Angela Duckworth
9. *Influence, New and Expanded: The Psychology of Persuasion* by Robert Cialdini
10. *Deep Work: Rules for Focused Success in a Distracted World* by Cal Newport

FAQ- CAREER IN MANAGEMENT ACCOUNTING

1. How does management accounting improve operational efficiencies, decrease operating costs and benefit senior leadership with decisions that impact product/service lines, mergers/acquisitions, and course corrections?
    - Management accountants build technical expertise in systems, processes, and tools to improve and access an organization's data. They then build relationships with business stakeholders to tie operational information to financials. With a holistic view, management accountants can raise awareness around decreasing efficiencies, increasing costs, and line profitability with other managers and executives to build and execute action plans to get the organization back on track.
    - As organizations face critical decisions, like whether to merge with another organization or not, management accountants prepare and build scenario planning models with a range of sensitivities based on what the business knows and assumes.

2. Where can management accounting knowledge be applied, and what can I do with a mastery of management accounting? Is there ease in transferring this skill across industries? What options exist should I want to pursue a different path mid-career?
    - Management accounting knowledge can be applied in a broad range of business support roles within finance, procurement, supply chain, and management. Management accountants build on a solid foundation of business knowledge and establish relationships to learn how the entire organization functions.
    - Mastery of management accounting opens many doors to a professional. They can either work as an expert individual contributor or advance in cost accounting, FP&A, or managerial roles.

    - For professionals interested in management accounting but didn't study accounting in college, one of the best paths is to pursue the CMA. The CMA prepares a candidate to understand the frameworks and methodologies used in cost accounting. The CMA is a highly-sought credential that will distinguish candidates in the job market once they're ready for a transition.
3. What can't or shouldn't a managerial accountant do? For example, a managerial accountant can tell a sales manager if the retail sales department shows a profit or not, but what are they expected to do after that? Is that their problem to solve?
    - Management accountants don't step into others' roles to drive profitability but instead follow the below route.
    - A management accountant's role is to provide sales updates and identify the drivers most contributing to the decrease in sales. They will spend time with the commercial team to get the story behind the numbers to determine if the results make sense. A management accountant will bring unexpected results to a sales manager's immediate attention and influence them to build a plan to reverse the trend.
    - A management accountant's work usually stops there. They will ask for updates from the sales manager and share that feedback with other managers and executives; they will attend meetings on the issue and ensure that plans are SMART and enacted.
4. What is management accounting? How is it different than financial accounting?
    - Management accounting is the foundation of every business. Professionals in this space provide vital information to decision-makers about how well they run their companies. Management accountants work closely with business operations to truly understand the drivers of the financials and provide insights, not facts and figures, to the people that matter.
    - Management accounting combines accounting, finance, and management with the leading-edge techniques to drive successful businesses.
    - Managerial accountants work within companies or organizations to manage and improve internal financial processes, accurately monitor costs while staying up-to-date with budget trends that may affect the bottom line, and assist company leaders by anticipating and forecasting needs before they arise.
    - Management accountants are sometimes confused with financial or public accountants, but clear distinctions exist. While all these professionals provide valuable services to an organization, the work and

responsibilities are very different. The distinction is that management accountants work within organizations, while public/financial accountants are external parties

- While financial accounting reports tend to be based on historical data, management reports are primarily forward-looking. Management accounting reports are also usually confidential and for internal use only, as opposed to financial accounting statements, which are publicly reported. Also, they are calculated based on generally accepted accounting practices based on management's informational needs instead of being calculated based on generally accepted accounting practices.

5. Is the CMA similar to the CGMA credential offered by an AICPA/CIMA partnership?
   - The CMA and CGMA are unrelated credentials. The CMA was first issued in 1972, while the CGMA was issued in 2012. Because of the declining interest in the CPA certification, the AICPA paired with the European-based CIMA to launch this credential in the US. To accelerate the CGMA's growth, the AICPA allowed every registered CPA in the US with 3 years of industry experience and a check for $150 to purchase the credential. The CMA, otherwise, must be earned through passing a rigorous 2-part examination. No CMA certification has ever been purchased. Since launching in the US in 2012, the CGMA has declined into relative obscurity, while the CMA has only become more valuable and prominent worldwide.
   - *https://www.goingconcern.com/get-your-cgma-designation-turd-gets-cold/*
   - *https://www.linkedin.com/pulse/dear-aicpa-i-wrote-your-concession-letter-ben-wann-cma-mba-cpa/*
6. What are some roles that a management accounting career can lead to?
   - A management accountant typically begins their career in an entry-level position as an internal auditor, cost accountant, or financial analyst. After a few years of experience, a management accountant may manage a team, become a financial controller, or advance as a specialized individual contributor. A few more years after that, they can become controllers for larger organizations, Head of FP&A, Director, VP, or CFO.
7. What does a management accountant do?
   - Management accountants analyze budgets, assess risks, and make strategic decisions based on internal financial data depending on their specific roles. The duties of a management accountant depend on their experience level. For example, an entry-level accountant typically

spends more time preparing reports, while a senior-level accountant is responsible for budget tracking and making decisions.

- Management accountants help formulate problem statements, identify how a decision will be made (i.e., identify the decision criteria), and begin acquiring and creating information needed. Part of accountants' job has always been – and always will be – recognizing information that must be acquired or developed (i.e., details the firm doesn't have but needs). However, part of the problem may be having too much information today and in the future. Accountants also need to recognize relevant information and when to use it.

8. What types of reports do management accountants prepare?
    - Management accountants generally prepare internal reports and analyses for business stakeholders, managers, and executives. There are standard and regular reports for metrics like inventory levels, line profitability, line efficiency, budget vs. actual costs, manufacturing variances, labor rates, and inventory at risk in any role.
    - Management accountants also provide ad-hoc analysis that is one-time or semi-regular. When business needs arise, management accountants must know where to find information and have the technical acumen to create a meaningful and dynamic analysis.
9. Do management accountants prepare financial statements? If so, which ones?
    - Management accountants also learn the basics of all three standard financial statements; the balance sheet, income statement, and statement of cash flows.
    - The CMA is especially valuable for learning the basics and applying this knowledge.
10. Do management accountants mentor and supervise accounting staff?
11. Do management accountants still need to be skilled in Microsoft Excel or have times changed? If so, what are key things to know about it?
    - Excel is the primary tool for analysis and reporting in nearly all management accounting roles. Excel has not remained static but has had significant upgrades in the last several years with Power Query and Power Pivot, which are crucial to automating and streamlining analytical processes. Not just familiarity but true expertise must be demonstrated to thrive in a modern cost accounting role.
    - The functions and tools below are used on a near-daily basis.
        - Data Validation

- Working in Excel
- Text to Columns
- Sumif
- Sumifs
- Countif(s)
- Vlookup
- Index
- Index-Match
- Pivot Tables
- Logical Operators
- Text Functions
- Data Tables
- Quick Access Tool Bar-Bonus
- Cell Formatting-Bonus
- Conditional Formatting-Bonus
- Indirect-Bonus
- Sumproduct-Bonus

12. My relatives all ask when I will get a CPA as a management accountant. Why does this happen? Should I do the CPA or the CMA? Or both?
    - Once upon a time, the CPA certification was more popular and well-known than the CMA. Generally, CPAs work in public practice for 3-5 years, working 60-80 hrs a week which essentially helps them earn 2 years of experience for every year a non-CPA would work. When these CPAs leave practice, as 80% do, they could transition into industry roles such as controller, director, or manager. It is here the correlation between highly-skilled professionals was established.
    - However, the CMA has become more prominent in the last two decades, and management accounting has a more impactful position. Professionals continuously learn and study to keep themselves on the cutting edge of best practices. Instead of CPAs competing against clerks for managerial roles, they must contend with CMAs who have just as much, if not more, training and years of industry experience to build upon.
    - In short, if you work in management accounting, the CMA should be the preferred credential to obtain for 90%+ candidates.
13. Is management accounting a rules-based or framework-based career?
    - Management accounting is a framework-based discipline, while financial accounting is a rules-based discipline. Depending on every question's circumstances, several variables help determine the right solution within various possibilities. Management accountants are valuable because they understand the balance between practicality and

compliance.

- Accountants must have a strong tolerance for and an ability to manage scenarios characterized by ambiguity and uncertainty. As the business environment grows in complexity, this skill will only increase in importance.

14. Do management accountants need to be skilled at communication?
    - Accountants need solid communication skills. As information engineers, accountants are liaisons between the firm's decision-makers and those responsible for the data analysis (e.g., other accountants, data scientists, statisticians, etc.). Communicating the information required and then interpreting that data and sharing results clearly is a critical skill.
15. What skillset within management accounting has emerged in the last 5 years and is in high demand?
    - Data analysis skills are in great demand. These skills – along with the ever-increasing availability of large quantities of data – influence other skills accountants will need to succeed in the future.
    - Controllership relies heavily on data for strategic insights, enhanced analytics, and more driver-based reporting frameworks, making data quality crucial to the function's performance. Many professionals face challenges compiling relevant, understandable, and effective data. Data's ever-increasing volume and complexities only intensify these hurdles.
    - Management accountants will play a leading role here by developing business acumen and assuming leadership roles to oversee enterprise data strategy, systems frameworks, and processes to meet the challenge and critical need to generate impactful data and reporting frameworks.
16. As a student, how can I get started with a career in management accounting?
    - For one, as an IMA Student member, you can learn about the role of accountants and financial managers in business and explore your career options.
    - The IMA offers student members access to many benefits of regular Professional membership at a significantly reduced rate. You must be enrolled in 6 or more credit hours at a college or university to qualify for this membership type.
    - Students who register can apply for CMA scholarships while still in school. It costs nothing to apply and provides an outstanding value. As you send out your resume during the hiring process, seeing that you are

currently studying for or have passed the CMA exam will indicate your high potential.

17. How much do management accountants typically earn? Is the field growing?
    - Median salary 2020: $73,560 per year
    - According to the U.S Bureau of Labor Statistics (BLS), accountants and auditors of all types have a promising future, with job prospects projected at a 7% growth rate through 2030.
18. Should I first pursue a master's degree, MBA, or CMA certification to excel in my management accounting career?
    - Many students are often tempted to continue their education after earning their bachelor's degrees. This could be the right or wrong decision, depending on the individual.
    - For most, finding employment upon graduation will be the best choice. With the cost of tuition leaving many students with debts to pay, it is wise to start working and paying these debts off early.
    - At the same time, much of the critical management accounting skills are learned on the job, not in school. Adding a master's or MBA degree will make more sense in the future once you have begun working and get a better understanding of your career interests.
    - Once you have completed your degree in accounting with a concentration in managerial accounting, you should consider working for at least 3-5 years before pursuing additional degrees. Many top MBA programs also prefer students with at least five years of work experience.
    - Some students who consider the dual CPA/CMA certifications may want to plan to earn at least 150 credits in their undergraduate degree to avoid the additional costs of a master's degree later. Check your state CPA regulations for further guidance here.
19. Do I need to be a math genius to succeed as a management accountant?
    - Short answer; yes. Long answer; no.
    - Mathematics is the science that deals with the logic of shape, quantity, and arrangement. Math is all around us in everything that we do. Math is a core building block for everything we experience daily, including mobile devices, architecture, art, money, engineering, and even sports. Math can be defined as using numbers and equations to solve a problem.
    - Accounting is recording financial transactions and storing, sorting, retrieving, summarizing, and presenting the results in various reports and analyses. For example, an accountant may be asked to run numbers and information

through a spreadsheet to determine how much revenue a company generated in a period and then compare that to the related expenses that determine income. These numbers are very exact, and the results need to be accurate enough to aid us in making good decisions.

- Management accountants are no longer required to be excellent at math because technological changes allow computers to do the heavy-lifting- Accountants must have average math skills. Today's accountant must still be grounded in the foundational principles of accounting. They must also understand the tools, logic, and methodologies behind the scenes while no longer having to perform the mathematical calculations behind each total and subtotal. A vital role of the accountant today is to identify the best tools to build robust processes that ensure that our inputs transform into the outputs that improve decision-making. Accountants today are more logic and systems-focused than they are on entering data into the systems.

20. How much money can I expect to earn as I advance in a management accounting career?
    - According to the IMA's 2021 Salary survey, the median salaries are as follows for years of experience.
    - The salary survey can be found here: *https://www.imanet.org/career-resources/salary-information?ssopc=1*
        - 1-5 yrs = $78,700
        - 6-10 yrs = $95,500
        - 11-15 yrs = $123,700
        - 16-20 yrs = $131,000
        - 21-25 yrs = $136,500
        - 26-30 yrs = $140,000
        - 31 and over = $146,640
        - Overall Median = $118,500

Made in the USA
Columbia, SC
28 October 2022